A New Owner's GUIDE TO AMERICAN ESKIMO DOGS

JG-132

Overleaf: An adult American Eskimo Dog and puppy.

Opposite page: An American Eskimo Dog from Circle B. Kennels in Texas.

The Publisher wishes to acknowledge the following owners of the dogs in this book: Heather Bailey, Barbara Blackwood, Pat Brabant, Royce and Jaqueline Brothers, Karla A. Cole, Ann DeTauvernier, Stuart and Helen Dick, Donna R. Hays, Nancy Hofman, Monika Hole, Sharon Janis, Chris Kerry, Lynn Martin, Roberta Martin, Phyllis A. Moore, Pam Neil, Tammy Nichols, Jan Palmar, Mr. And Mrs. Gordon E. Patterson, Cindy Robbins, Karen Sherba, Sharon Shroeder, Rosemary Stevens, Sandy Tocco, Shirley Tooker, and Tracey Vitteetoe.

Photographers: Heather Bailey, Richard Beauchamp, Barbara Blackwood, Pat Brabant, Jenifer Brimmer, Royce and Jaqueline Brothers, Carlson Studio, Karla A. Cole, Ann DeTauvernier, Stuart and Helen Dick, Isabelle Francais, Donna R. Hays, Nancy Hofman, Monika Hole, Sharon Janis, Chris Kerry, Lynn Martin, Roberta Martin, Phyllis A. Moore, Pam Neil, Tammy Nichols, Sara Nugent, Jan Palmar, Mr. And Mrs. Gordon E. Patterson, Cindy Robbins, Karen Sherba, Sharon Shroeder, Rosemary Stevens, Karen Taylor, Sandy Tocco, Shirley Tooker, and Tracey Vitteetoe.

The author acknowledges the contribution of Judy Iby for the following chapters in this book: Sport of Purebred Dogs, Health Care, Identification and Finding the Lost Dog, Traveling with Your Dog, and Behavior and Canine Communication.

The portrayal of canine pet products in this book is for general instructive value only; the appearance of such products does not necessarily constitute an endorsement by the authors, the publisher, or the owners of the dogs portrayed in this book.

Dedication: To the devoted friends and fanciers of the American Eskimo Dog and particularly to Helen Dick, Rosemary Stevens, and Lynn Martin Wyza, whose love of the breed and special insight helped make this book possible.

© by T.F.H. Publications, Inc.

Distributed in the UNITED STATES to the Pet Trade by T.F.H. Publications, Inc., One T.F.H. Plaza, Neptune City, NJ 07753; on the Internet at www.tfh.com; in CANADA Rolf C. Hagen Inc., 3225 Sartelon St. Laurent-Montreal Quebec H4R 1E8; Pet Trade by H & L Pet Supplies Inc., 27 Kingston Crescent, Kitchener, Ontario N2B 2T6; in ENGLAND by T.F.H. Publications, PO Box 15, Waterlooville PO7 6BQ; in AUSTRALIA AND THE SOUTH PACIFIC by T.F.H. (Australia), Pty. Ltd., Box 149, Brookvale 2100 N.S.W., Australia; in NEW ZEALAND by Brooklands Aquarium Ltd. 5 McGiven Drive, New Plymouth, RD1 New Zealand; in SOUTH AFRICA, Rolf C. Hagen S.A. (PTY.) LTD. P.O. Box 201199, Durban North 4016, South Africa; in Japan by T.F.H. Publications, Japan—Jiro Tsuda, 10-12-3 Ohjidai, Sakura, Chiba 285, Japan. Published by T.F.H. Publications, Inc.
MANUFACTURED IN THE
UNITED STATES OF AMERICA
BY T.F.H. PUBLICATIONS, INC.

A New Owner's
Guide to
AMERICAN ESKIMO
DOGS

Richard G. Beauchamp

Contents

1998 Edition

The American Eskimo Dog's loving and happy disposition makes him the ideal family pet.

This lovely pair of American Eskimo puppies pose for posterity.

The versatile and athletic American Eskimo Dog excels in agility competition.

The American Eskimo Dog is famous for his lovely "smile."

This inquisitive Eskie stops for a chance to sniff the tulips.

FOREWORD

Like most children in elementary school I spent September through May daydreaming about the impending summer vacation. No homework or long dreary days in the classroom, just long carefree days with my neighborhood friends. However, most of my summer dreams centered on the one month of each year that my cousins and I spent at our grandparents farm in northern Michigan. It doesn't take a great deal of imagination to picture what these magical 30 days meant to children born and raised in the city.

There were many wonderful moments in those summers of the 1940s, but Saturday nights were always the high point of each week. On that night Grandpa Miller would load us all into his ancient Model-T Ford truck and take us into town for the outdoor movie. The movie was great, but it was the opening act of each Saturday night that kept us enthralled.

The proprietors of the outdoor event were the Muellers, a couple

Ch. Pinebrook Walker's Windstar and Windsong at 13 weeks of age.

who had immigrated to the United States from Europe just prior to World War II. They had owned and traveled with a small circus throughout Germany and the middle European countries. When the Muellers were forced to flee their home there was no choice but to leave everything behind. They escaped with seven small white dogs that made up the circus troop called "Hans and Maria Mueller's Wonder Dogs."

The little white dogs danced and clowned on their hind legs, wearing top hats and spangled costumes. They jumped

Lights, camera, action! Looks like this Eskie is ready for show business.

through hoops and even played tricks on their trainers. Quite frankly, we could have watched the amazing Spitz dogs all night long.

We returned one summer to find Mr. Mueller had died during the previous winter and his wife had disbanded the little act. Mrs. Mueller had kept two of the dogs herself, but the rest had gone to live with other townspeople. We tracked some of them down in their new homes and were delighted to find several litters of puppies. As only grandchildren are able to do, we convinced our grandparents they were in desperate need of one of these "wonder dogs."

Every year until we were too old to spend a summer month on the farm, we worked on our Spitz dog Snowball's repertoire of tricks. We had collectively decided that when the canine whiz kid's puppies came, which never did happen, and she became the world's first talking dog, we would open our own circus. Fantasizing about running away with my own circus was sometimes the only thing that made the endless months in school bearable.

Sadly, my cousins dropped out of our summer idyll one by one as they pursued more sophisticated interests. Snowball and I were left to prepare for our circus act alone. Though a bit lonely, I was the circus ringmaster for three summers running!

Then one summer I arrived at the farm, but there was no Snowball. She had gone to her own "big circus in the sky," as my grandmother put it. It seemed my dream of fame under the big top was never to be realized.

Many years had passed during which my interest in dogs led me to become a breeder, exhibitor, all-breed judge, and dog writer. Every time I would see a Spitz my memories would go rushing back to those wonderful Michigan summers.

In 1980, while judging a rare breed show in Southern California, I was approached by Lila and Leroy Bean. As members of the California American Eskimo Association, they asked me to serve an apprenticeship and become a judge of their breed. To my great delight I was to find that the Eskies were one and the same breed as Snowball and the Spitz dogs of my childhood.

Since that day I have been very involved with the American Eskimo Dog and have stood in admiration of the dedicated

With those bright eyes and happy expressions, is it any wonder that Eskie puppies inspire people to fall in love at first sight?

owners and breeders throughout the country. I have not only had the distinct pleasure of judging the breed throughout the United States, but I have also had the opportunity to observe and compare the breed with its Spitz cousins throughout the world. I have also been able to put my observations and experience to use in breed standard clarifications and judges' educational presentations.

An eight-week-old puppy from Kandia Kennels.

It is my hope that *A New Owner's Guide to American Eskimo Dogs* will help to develop an appreciation for the breed's many attributes, as well as foster further national interest in the breed. I also wish to share my own knowledge and experience with those who already love American Eskimos and those who do not yet know them well.

The magical relationship between a properly socialized American Eskimo puppy and a child will be one that lasts a lifetime.

HISTORY and Origin of the American Eskimo Dog

"Beauty without vanity, strength without insolence and all the virtues of man without his vices."

It is said that Lord Byron wrote these beautiful words about the American Eskimo Dog, which was known as the Spitz during his time. Anyone who owns or loves the American Eskimo will assure you that those words are true. Although we will never be sure of the inspiration for Byron's words, the American Eskimo Dog fits his description in both form and character, proving that the history of the American Eskimo Dog traces back into antiquity.

IN THE BEGINNING

The domesticated dog of today descends from *Canis lupis*, the wolf. In fact, most dog breeds can be traced to a particular type of wolf from the north, known as the Northern European Gray Wolf. No one is quite sure how long it took for the wolf to move out of the forest and into man's cave dwellings. However, it seems obvious that observation of the wolf could easily have taught early man some effective hunting techniques that he would have been able to use to his advantage. Also, many of the wolf's social habits probably seemed strikingly familiar to early man. It also became increasingly obvious as the man-wolf relationship developed through the ages that certain descendants of these increasingly domesticated wolves could assist man in pursuits other than hunting, such as hauling and warning when a marauding neighbor or beast of prey threatened.

Through the centuries dogs have evolved and changed drastically due to man's intervention. However, long before man began to manipulate the size and shape of *Canis familiaris* (the domestic dog) there existed a branch of the family *Canidae* that retained many of the wolf's physical characteristics. Like their undomesticated ancestors, these dogs maintained the characteristics that protected them from

The beautiful and athletic American Eskimo Dog is believed to be a direct descendant of the German Spitz.

the rugged environment of northern Europe. Weather-resistant coats protected them from rain and cold. Plumed tails could cover and protect the nose and mouth should the animal be forced to sleep in the snow. Small prick ears were not easily frostbitten or frozen. The muzzle had sufficient length to warm the frigid air before it reached the lungs. Leg length was sufficient to keep the chest and abdomen above the snow line. Tails were carried horizontally or up over the back rather than trailing behind in the snow.

The skeletal remains of these early wolf descendants have been found throughout northern and central Europe, northern Asia, and the Arctic regions of North America. It is believed that these animals stand as the forefathers of what are now commonly referred to as the Arctic or Nordic breeds. This group can be divided into four categories: hunting dogs, such as Norwegian Elkhound and Chow Chow; draft dogs, like the Alaskan Malamute and Siberian Husky; herding dogs, like the Samoyed; and companion dogs, which

These are two white Giant Spitz dogs photographed by the author in Germany. It is easy to see how similar they are to the American Eskimo Dog of today.

include most of the Spitz-type dogs, such as the German Spitz, Japanese Spitz, and the American Eskimo.

In particular, the remains of one specific branch of the family *Canidae*, *Canis familiaris palustris*, otherwise known as the dog of the lake, have been found in many places throughout northern Europe. These dogs are said to have existed in the late Stone Age. Although their exact role in the lives of the nomadic peoples will never be fully understood, American Eskimo Dog author, enthusiast, and breed historian Nancy J. Hoffman suggests they may have served as guard dogs—sounding the alarm by barking when danger threatened. The alert nature, rapid vocal response, and protective devotion to home and hearth of the Spitz breeds of today definitely support this belief.

THE SPITZ BREEDS IN GERMANY

The Spitz breeds had already became popular in Germany in the early 1500s. Count Eberhard zu Sayne, a baron who resided in Germany's Rhine Valley, is the first person credited with referring to the dogs as Spitz. The word Spitz is German for "sharp point." The count described the dogs as having no real interest in hunting but being totally dedicated to their master and to protecting their home and

The courageous American Eskimo Dog is well known for her steady temperament and loyalty to her master.

property. Evidently, the Count had great influence in Germany because from his first use of the term Spitz in 1540, the word was included in the German vocabulary and in dictionaries.

Spitz dogs came in many sizes and colors, each being identified by a separate name. However, they all shared the same physical characteristics that had distinguished them for many centuries. Historically, dog breeds and varieties within breeds have been developed in the various towns and villages of Europe and Great Britain quite simply through the color and size preferences of influential individuals. Varieties in the different areas often took on the name of the towns or villages in which they were developed. Sometimes the name referred to the particular duties assigned to the dogs. At other times the breed or variety's name was the result of the town or province in which the breed was developed. For our purposes it is probably most useful to divide the German Spitz varieties by size. This type of classification was originally used in Germany and is still used today by the Federacion Internationale Cynologique, the canine governing authority of Europe.

The Wolfspitz is the largest of the five German Spitz breeds. It stands approximately 18 or more inches at the shoulder. The only color permitted by the standard is gray. It is believed that the Keeshond descended from this animal. The next largest is the Gross Spitz or Giant Spitz, which stands 16 inches or slightly larger at the shoulder. The Giant Spitz is most often seen in white, black, brown, and orange. The Mittelspitze or Standard Spitz is ideally 11 to 14 inches high at the shoulders and can be white, black, brown, wolf gray, or orange. The Kleinspitz or Small Spitz is white, black, brown, wolf gray, or orange and measures 8 $^1/_2$ to 11 inches at the shoulder. The Zwergspitz or Dwarf Spitz is white, black, brown, wolf gray, or orange and measures less than 8 $^1/_2$ inches. While size and color separate the Spitz varieties in Germany, it should be remembered that they continued to retain similar features.

The White Spitz enjoyed great popularity both in Germany and abroad. By the 1700s it was the popular dog of British society. The dogs were a particular favorite of Queen Charlotte, who was born in Germany and remembered the dogs from her childhood home. Charlotte had obtained her dogs from the area around Pomerania, which at that time was known for the breeding of exceptional white dogs. Charlotte eventually began referring to the white Spitz as Pomeranians and a breed name was born.

Pomeranians gained popularity, even among England's commoners in the 1800s. The dogs weighed about 20 to 30 pounds and were about 18 inches at the shoulder. Their size and color was approximately the same as today's Standard Variety American Eskimo. However, later we will see that the Miniature Variety of the Eskie is actually tied more closely to the Pomeranian than the Standard.

The ascent of Queen Victoria to the British throne was to change the character of the Pomeranian forever. While traveling though Italy, Victoria, an avid dog fancier, found a red sable Spitz that weighed only 12 pounds. She called him Marco, and upon her return to Great Britain he became her constant companion.

Donna Hays's Ch. Diamon's Bewitching Sabrina is taking her all-American name to heart.

Victoria exhibited him at dog shows in London as a Pomeranian and little Marco created a minor sensation, launching a demand for "Pomeranians" of his size and color. For a time, both the larger white and smaller colored dogs were shown simultaneously. However, in the face of the smaller colored variety's popularity the white dogs fell from favor. From that point on the diminutive colored variety Spitz dog became known as the Pomeranian.

THE AMERICAN ESKIMO GETS HIS NAME

By the turn of the century the Spitz had found its way to America, probably on board ships full of early German settlers. Unfortunately, many of these early dogs were somewhat sharp in temperament and not considered entirely trustworthy.

In the early 1900s, Mr. and Mrs. James Hall had become involved in breeding the White Spitz in what they called American Eskimo Kennels. This was simply the name of their kennel and had nothing to do with the dogs the kennel actually housed. The Halls contacted the United Kennel Club in 1913 and negotiated to have their Spitz dogs registered with the organization.

How the breed came to be known as the American Eskimo Dog remains a mystery. Some believe it was simply because the Halls did not like or understand the meaning of the German word "Spitz." Others think they simply opted for the name of their kennel even though it had absolutely nothing to do with the breed.

However, another story may well have been closer to the truth. Because of the world political situation, American sentiments were dramatically anti-German at the time the Halls applied for recognition of the breed. So much so, that German Shepherd Dogs came to be referred to as Alsatians and Dachshunds were referred to as Badger Dogs. Americans wanted nothing to do with anything associated with Germany. American Eskimo was far more patriotic sounding than the Germanic sounding "Spitz."

The first known breed standard for the American Eskimo was credited to Dr. E. G. Fuhrman, then president of the United Kennel Club. Although it basically described the breed as it appears today, it contained some gross errors, including a statement that the Eskie was a miniature version of the Samoyed.

In 1913 the UKC first admitted the American Eskimo to its stud books and continued to do so until 1970. During this time the UKC accepted "single dog registrations," that is, a dog of obvious pure breeding could be registered without benefit of a pedigree. However, the studbooks of the United Kennel Club have been closed to single dog registrations of the American Eskimo since 1970. While single dog registry may seem unusual, many kennel clubs of the world have resorted to the same procedure when trying to establish foundation stock for a new breed or to re-establish a breed decimated by war or genetic problems.

In November, 1969, 43 American Eskimo fanciers from across the country gathered in DeSota, Missouri, and formed the National American Eskimo Dog Association. Thomas

The first American Eskimo Dog arrived in America at the turn of the century. This beautiful litter is owned and bred by Karla A. Cole.

The American Eskimo Dog attained full status as a member of the American Kennel Club's Non-Sporting Group in July of 1995.

Maxwell was elected president of the new organization. He became one of the breed's staunchest supporters and remained in office for many years. Mr. Maxwell's female Standard Eskie, Maxwell's Gidget, became the first champion in the breed, and another dog of his breeding, Maxwell's Zsa Zsa, became the first Miniature champion. Mr. and Mrs. Maxwell bred many champions and traveled extensively showing their dogs throughout the US.

Today, chapters of the American Eskimo Dog Association exist throughout the United States. Shows are held around the country on almost every weekend of the year under the sanction of the United Kennel Club. It is a credit to the breeders and members of the AEDA that the Eskie's temperament has been so greatly improved that they are now considered to be among the finest family dogs available.

On April 13, 1993, the Board of Directors of the American Kennel Club voted to accept the American Eskimo Dog into its stud book. The breed was shown in the miscellaneous classes of American Kennel Club shows until July 1, 1995, at which time Eskies attained full breed status as a member of the Non-Sporting Group. The American Eskimo Dog Club of America is the AKC Parent Club.

CHARACTERISTICS of the American Eskimo Dog

RESPONSIBLE DOG OWNERSHIP

If you haven't decided whether or not to add an American Eskimo puppy to your family, a visit to the kennel of a breeder will undoubtedly settle the matter once and for all—you will not leave without one! Eskie puppies are simply irresistible. It is for this very reason that you should give serious thought to the final decision. All puppies are cuddly and cute. However, it is important to remember that they are living, breathing, mischievous little creatures that are entirely dependent upon their owner for everything once they leave their mother.

Buying a dog before you are absolutely sure that you want to make the kind of commitment that is involved can be a serious mistake. The prospective dog owner must clearly understand the amount of time and work involved in dog ownership. Failure to understand the requirements of dog ownership is one of the main reasons there are so

A litter of Eskie puppies may be irresistible, but be certain to educate yourself about the responsibilities of owning a dog before you bring one home.

18

The American Eskimo Dog has a number of unique qualities that make him a versatile and amiable pet. Circle B Jay Bar's Sterling Explorer and Son of a Gun enjoy a stroll through the Texas bluebells.

many unwanted canines whose lives end in animal shelters.

Before contemplating the purchase of any dog, there are some very basic questions that must be answered. Most important, does the person who will ultimately be responsible for the dog's care and well-being actually want a dog? All too often it is the mother of the household who must shoulder the responsibility of the family dog's day-to-day care. While the rest of the family may be wildly enthusiastic about having a dog, perhaps they are away most of the day at school or work. It is often mom who will be taking on the additional responsibility of caring for the family dog.

Pets are a wonderful method of teaching children responsibility, but the enthusiasm that inspires children to promise anything in order to have a new puppy may quickly wane. Who will take care of the puppy once the novelty wears off?

Desire to own a dog aside, does the lifestyle of the family actually provide for responsible dog ownership? If the entire family is away from early morning to late at night, who will provide for all of the puppy's needs? It is difficult to meet the feeding and exercise requirements of a puppy if no one is home.

It is also important to consider whether or not the breed of dog you are considering is suitable for the lifestyle you live. When you consider an Eskie you have several options because there are several different sizes: Standard, Miniature, and Toy. A full-grown Standard-size Eskie can handle the rough and tumble play of young children, while a very young Toy-size Eskie cannot.

Then, there is the matter of hair. A luxuriously coated dog is certainly beautiful to behold, but all that hair takes a great deal of care. Brushing an adult Eskie requires time and patience. Long-haired dogs shed their coats in the home. Naturally, the longer the hair, the more noticeable it will be.

As great as claims are for any breed's intelligence and trainability, remember that the new dog must be taught every household rule that he is to observe. Some dogs catch on more quickly than others, and puppies are just as inclined to forget or disregard lessons as young human children.

CASE FOR THE PUREBRED DOG

As previously mentioned, all puppies are cute. But not all puppies grow up to be particularly attractive adults. What is considered to be beautiful by one person is not necessarily seen as attractive by another. It is almost impossible to determine what a mixed breed puppy will look like as an adult. Nor will it be possible to determine if the mixed breed puppy's temperament is suitable for the person or family who wishes to own him. If the puppy grows up to be too big, too hairy, or too active for the owner, then what will happen to him?

Size and temperament can vary to a degree even within purebred dogs. However, selective breeding over many generations has produced dogs that give the would-be owner reasonable insurance of what the purebred puppy will look and act like as an adult. Aesthetics completely aside, this predictability is more important than one might think.

Purebred puppies will grow up to look like their adult relatives and will behave pretty much like the rest of their family. Any dog, mixed breed or not, has the potential to be a loving companion. However, the predictability of a purebred dog offers reasonable insurance that he will not only suit the owner's lifestyle but the person's aesthetic demands as well.

Before you bring an Eskie into your household, visit breeders and spend as much time with both puppies and adults as you can. Be sure that the Eskie is the dog that appeals to you aesthetically and temperamentally.

Dedicated Eskie breeders are careful to be true to the breed's original character and purpose. This Circle B youngster is a lovely example.

WHO SHOULD OWN AN ESKIE?

What kind of person should own an Eskie? In a word, the Eskie owner must be *dedicated*. Your

dog will be totally and completely dedicated to you and that dedication must be rewarded in kind.

Don't forget, the Eskie is a long-coated white breed that requires your care and attention. Although many valid claims are made for the easy care of the Eskie coat, the breed is heavy coated, white, and does shed. If you appreciate the look of the breed, do realize it will take some time and effort on your part to kept it looking that way.

While the Eskie can be an ideal choice for the person with allergy problems, it must be remembered that the breed, like many all-white and pink-skinned dogs, can be extremely sensitive to fleas. Unless carefully controlled, flea bites can and will lead to severe scratching. Incessant scratching results in skin eruptions and "hot spots," which are accompanied by hair loss.

Just because the Eskie is totally dedicated to you, do not think for a moment that you will have a dog that obeys mindlessly. An Eskie must have a "boss." The breed is most secure when it is given boundaries and when the boundaries are consistently

The American Eskimo Dog's loving and happy disposition make him a welcome addition to most families. Michael Brooks and his puppy certainly agree!

22

enforced. Your Eskie must start understanding household rules from the first moment that he enters your home. To accomplish this it will take patience, dedication, and a firm but gentle hand.

Someone who needs a dog that does well living outdoors with minimal owner interaction should look to another breed. The Eskie must have constant human companionship and social interaction, not only with his owner but with all kinds of people and other dogs. The Eskie raised without this socialization can easily become introverted and difficult to handle.

The young Eskie can pass through an adolescent stage during which he decides that his owner or family is all that is necessary for his well-being. Without the benefit of socialization, the youngster can become very antisocial— unless he is made to understand that this behavior is unacceptable. It is then up to the caring owner to help guide the Eskie through this difficult stage. Patience, persistence, and support will help your Eskie through this awkward time, but it does take a commitment to stay out there with the "bashful" youngster.

Look at that face! Whether male or female, the Eskie will make an equally loving, devoted, and trainable companion.

If you are willing to make the necessary commitment that an Eskie requires, let me assure you there are few breeds that are more versatile, devoted, and adaptable. Do not forget the Eskie heritage—devoted companion, protector of his human family and their household.

THE ESKIE PERSONALITY

Historically, the American Eskimo Dog has been a close companion to man. Whether a favorite of the royal family or a circus performer, everything the Eskie has done has been done in the company of his human family. In order to fully develop his many admirable characteristics, the breed is happiest when allowed to continue that association. As was previously mentioned, this is not a breed to be relegated to kennel life or an outdoor run with only occasional access to your life and environment. The very essence of the Eskie is his personality and devoted nature, which are best developed by constant human contact.

The Eskie owner must be prepared for the fact that the breed is intent upon protecting his home and his human family from any impending danger or harm. The best way an Eskie can do this is to warn you when he perceives the possibility of anything threatening the safety of his owners. This is accomplished by barking—sounding the alarm to give you a warning.

Barking is a characteristic typical of all the Spitz breeds, particularly the American Eskimo. It is important that your Eskie learns the difference between necessary and unnecessary barking. The latter can be nerve wracking to an owner and a nuisance to neighbors. Eskies are smart dogs and quickly learn barking boundaries if strictly enforced. Do remember, however, the warning bark is a part of the Eskie heritage. It is up to the owner to make sure that their Eskie understands when and where barking is appropriate.

Although the American Eskimo is certainly not a vindictive breed, we are never surprised to hear that an Eskie who has been completely housebroken will suddenly forget all his manners or become destructive in protest of suddenly being left alone too often or too long. Some Eskies will let you know they are not getting the attention they need by destroying household items, particularly those things that belong to the individual the dog particularly misses.

This does not mean that you must be home all day long to cater to the whims of your Eskie. Many Eskies are owned by working people who are away a good part of the day. The dogs are well mannered and trustworthy when left home alone. The key here is the quality of time, rather than quantity, spent with an Eskie. Morning or evening walks, grooming sessions, regular training routines, and consistent rule enforcement are vital to the breed's personality development and attitude. Eskies live to be talked to and praised by their owners.

Everything about the Eskie's personality indicates that it is a non-aggressive breed. At the same time, though, the breed has an inherent wariness of strangers. Again, we cannot dismiss the breed's history—guardian of the household. Still, it would be totally out of character for an Eskie to challenge his owner on any point regardless of how much he might object to what he is being asked to do.

This is not to say that an Eskie is beyond testing your patience or the reality of the boundaries you set. The breed can be very headstrong and may well act as though it has not heard your command. It may take sitting your Eskie down, looking him in the eye, and repeating your command. A stern and disapproving voice, combined with consistency in enforcing the rules, is usually more than sufficient to let an American Eskimo know you disapprove of what he is doing. It is never necessary to strike your Eskie in any circumstance. A sharp "No!" is normally more than it takes to make your point.

Although it may take time and patience, your American Eskimo Dog is very intelligent and can be trained to do anything. This Eskie obviously excels in agility competition.

The Eskie makes a great effort to please his owner and is highly trainable as long as the trainer is not heavy handed. Any training problems encountered are usually due to the owner rather than the Eskie's lack of understanding or inability to learn.

Some Eskie owners think of their companions as "little people" and unwittingly spoil their dogs until they become nuisances. It must be understood that the American Eskimo is first and foremost a dog. Dogs, like their wolf ancestors, are pack animals in need of a "pack leader." Your Eskie is dependent upon you to provide that leadership. When that leadership is not provided an Eskie can easily become confused and neurotic.

Setting boundaries is important for your Eskie's well-being as well as his relationship with you. As we mentioned earlier, the American Eskimo is not vindictive or stubborn if properly trained, but the breed does need guidance in order to achieve its potential.

STANDARD for the American Eskimo Dog

The American Eskimo Dog enjoys the benefit of being eligible for showing at both American Kennel Club and United Kennel Club shows. While the standards of the breed are generally the same, there are subtle differences that the Eskie owner should be aware of should he or she plan to show at one or another of the organization's licensed shows. We therefore present both of the standards.

OFFICIAL AMERICAN KENNEL CLUB STANDARD FOR THE AMERICAN ESKIMO DOG

General Appearance—The American Eskimo Dog, a loving companion dog, presents a picture of strength and agility, alertness and beauty. It is a small

The American Eskimo Dog is a loving companion dog and presents a picture of strength, agility, alertness, and beauty. This Eskie is owned by Royce and Jaqueline Brothers of Circle B Kennels in Texas.

to medium-size Nordic type dog, always white, or white with biscuit cream. The American Eskimo Dog is compactly built and well balanced, with good substance, and an alert, smooth gait. The face is Nordic type with erect triangular shaped ears, and distinctive black points (lips, nose, and eye rims). The white double coat consists of a short, dense undercoat, with a longer guard hair growing through it forming the outer coat, which is straight with no curl or wave. The coat is thicker and longer around the neck and chest forming a lion-like ruff,

which is more noticeable on dogs than on bitches. The rump and hind

Even as a puppy the American Eskimo Dog should exhibit some of the qualities of the breed standard.

legs down to the hocks are also covered with thicker, longer hair forming the characteristic breeches. The richly plumed tail is carried loosely on the back.

Size, Proportion, Substance–*Size.* There are three separate size divisions of the American Eskimo Dog (all measurements are heights at withers): Toy, 9 inches to and including 12 inches; Miniature, over 12 inches to and including 15 inches; and Standard, over 15 inches to and including 19 inches. There is no preference for size within each division. *Disqualification: Under 9 inches or over 19 inches. Proportion.* Length of back from point of shoulder to point of buttocks is slightly greater than height at withers, an approximate 1.1 to 1 ratio. *Substance.* The American Eskimo Dog is strong and compactly built with adequate bone.

Head–*Expression* is keen, intelligent, and alert. *Eyes* are not fully round, but slightly oval. They should be set well apart, and not slanted, prominent or bulging. Tear stain, unless severe, is not to be faulted. Presence of tear stain should not outweigh consideration of type, structure, or temperament. Dark to medium brown is the preferred eye color. Eye rims are black to dark brown. Eyelashes are white. Faults: amber eye color or pink eye rims. *Disqualification: blue eyes. Ears* should conform to head size and be triangular, slightly blunt-tipped, held erect, set on high yet well apart, and blend softly with the head. *Skull* is slightly crowned and softly wedge-shaped, with widest breadth between the ears. The stop is well defined, although not abrupt. The *muzzle* is broad, with length not exceeding the length of the skull, although it may be

The American Eskimo Dog should have a white, or white with biscuit cream, colored coat.

slightly shorter. *Nose* pigment is black to dark brown. *Lips* are thin and tight, black to dark brown in color. Faults: pink nose pigment or pink lip pigment. The *jaw* should be strong with a full complement of close fitting teeth. The *bite* is scissors, or pincer.

Neck, Topline, Body—The *neck* is carried proudly erect, well set on, medium in length, and in a strong, graceful arch. The *topline* is level. The *body* of the American Eskimo Dog is strong and compact, but not cobby. The chest is deep and broad with well-sprung ribs. Depth of chest extends approximately to point of elbows.

The Eskie's coat consists of a short, dense undercoat, with long hair growing through it to form the outer coat, which is straight with no curl or wave.

Slight tuck-up of belly just behind the ribs. The back is straight, broad, level, and muscular. The loin is strong and well-muscled. The American Eskimo Dog is neither too long nor too short coupled. The *tail* is set moderately high and reaches approximately to the point of hock when down. It is carried loosely on the back, although it may be dropped when at rest.

Forequarters— are well angulated. The shoulder is firmly set and has adequate muscle but is not overdeveloped. The shoulder blades are well laid back and slant 45 with the horizontal. At the point of shoulder the shoulder blade forms an approximate right angle with the upper arm. The legs are parallel and straight to the pasterns. The pasterns are strong and flexible with a slant of about 20. Length of leg in proportion to the body. Dewclaws on the front legs may be removed at the owner's discretion; if present, they are not to be faulted. Feet are oval, compact, tightly knit and well padded with hair. Toes are well arched. Pads are black to dark brown, tough and deeply cushioned. Toenails are white.

Hindquarters—Hindquarters are well angulated. The lay of the pelvis is approximately 30 to the horizontal. The upper thighs are well developed. Stifles are well bent. Hock joints are well let down and firm. The rear pasterns are straight. Legs are parallel from the rear and turn neither in nor out. Feet are as described for the front legs. Dewclaws are not present on the hind legs.

Coat–The American Eskimo Dog has a stand-off, double coat consisting of a dense undercoat and a longer coat of guard hair growing through it to form the outer coat. It is straight with no curl or wave. There is a pronounced ruff around the neck which is more noticeable on dogs than bitches. Outer part of the ear should be well covered with short, smooth hair, with longer tufts of hair growing in front of ear openings. Hair on muzzle should be short and smooth. The backs of the front legs should be well feathered, as are the rear legs down to the hock. The tail is covered profusely with long hair. THERE IS TO BE NO TRIMMING OF THE WHISKERS OR BODY COAT AND SUCH TRIMMING WILL BE SEVERELY PENALIZED. The only permissible trimming is to neaten the feet and the backs of the rear pasterns.

Color–Pure white is the preferred color, although white with biscuit cream is permissible. Presence of biscuit cream should not outweigh consideration of type, structure, or temperament. The skin of the American Eskimo Dog is pink or gray. *Disqualification: any color other than white or biscuit cream.*

Gait–The American Eskimo Dog shall trot, not pace. The gait is agile, bold, well balanced, and frictionless, with good forequarter reach and good hindquarter drive. As speed increases, the American Eskimo Dog will single track with the legs converging toward the center line of gravity while the back remains firm, strong, and level.

Temperament–The American Eskimo Dog is intelligent, alert, and friendly, although slightly conservative. It is never overly shy nor aggressive, and such dogs are to be severely penalized in the show ring. At home it is an excellent watchdog, sounding a warning bark to announce the arrival of

any stranger. It is protective of its home and family, although it

The American Eskimo Dog is compactly built, with good substance and an alert, smooth gait.

The American Eskimo Dog is intelligent, alert, and friendly, although slightly conservative at first. does not threaten to bite or attack people. The American Eskimo Dog learns new tasks quickly and is eager to please.

DISQUALIFICATIONS

Any color other than white or biscuit cream
Blue Eyes
Height: under 9 or over 19.
Approved: October 11, 1994
Effective: November 30, 1994

OFFICIAL UNITED KENNEL CLUB STANDARD FOR THE AMERICAN ESKIMO DOG

General Appearance: The American Eskimo is a well-balanced, typical model of a northern working type dog. The body is proportioned and balanced. Back length from point of shoulder to root of tail should equal the height from pad to top of withers. The face is Nordic type with triangular ears which are slightly rounded at tips and readily distinguished black points (nose, lips, and eye rims). Has an alert, smooth carriage.

The American Eskimo Dog is protective of his home and family, learns new tasks quickly, and is eager to please. The coat should be thick especially around the neck, forepart of shoulders and chest forming a lion-like mane. The rump and hind legs down to the hock are also thickly coated forming the characteristic trousers. The ruff (mane) and long outer guard hairs are more prominent on males than females. The richly plumed tail is carried over the back. They should present a picture of beauty, alertness, strength and agility.

Head: One denoting power, being wedge-shaped with broad, slightly crowned skull. Head size should be in proportion to body. The stop should not be abrupt but well defined.

Muzzle: In proportion to the head, medium in length, and covered with smooth, short hairs.

32

Ears: Should conform to head size, slightly rounded at tips, triangular, held erect, set well apart and covered inside with hair. Ears should be blend softly with the wedge shape head. Outer part of ears to be covered with smooth, short hairs, longer tufts of hair in front of the ear openings. Color inside the ear should be pink or slight tinge of gray.

Eyes: Should be slightly oval and not slanted. Should be black to brown, set well apart with intelligent expression. Eye rims should be black for preference but dark brown is permissible. Eyelashes should be white.

Nose: Leather black to dark brown.

Lips: Black to dark brown, saggy flews are objectionable.

Teeth and Jaw: Strong jaw with close fitting teeth meeting in a level to scissors bite. A full compliment of sound teeth is preferred.

The Eskie's plume tail is set high and carried loosely over his back.

Neck: Medium in length and in proportion to body, strong, carried proudly erect, blending into shoulders with graceful arch.

Body: Strong and compactly built but not too short coupled. Back Length from point of shoulder to root of tail should equal the height from pad to top of withers. In the male, both testicles must be in the scrotum.

Chest and Ribs: Should be strong, show broadness and depth. Depth of chest should be approximate point of elbows. Ribs should be well-sprung and begin upsweep behind the ninth rib to insure adequate room for heart and lung action. Heart and lung room are secured more by body depth than width. Belly should be slightly tucked up immediately behind the ribs.

Back and Loins: Should be straight, level, broad and muscular. Loins should be well muscled and not so short as to interfere with easy rhythmic movement and powerful drive of back legs. Females may be slightly longer in back.

Forequarters: Front legs should be parallel and straight to the pasterns, elbows close to the body and turned neither in nor out. Pastern should be strong and flexible to add spring to movement. Length of leg should be proportioned to body size for a total even balance. Shoulder should have a 45 degree lay back and be firmly set. Front legs well feathered on back side. Dewclaws may be removed at the owner's option.

Hindquarters: Upper thighs should be well developed and muscled. Stifles approximately 30 degree lay off pelvis, hocks well let down and sharply defined. Hind legs should be parallel when viewed from the rear in a natural stance, they should be parallel when viewed from the rear in a natural stance, they should turn neither in nor out. Dewclaws are objectionable on hind legs and should be removed for the dog's own safety. The hind legs should be muscular and of adequate bone to blend with body size; the dog should not appear clumsy or racy.

Feet: Should be oval in shape, compact, well padded with hair. Pads should be tough and deeply cushioned. Feet should neither "toe in" nor "out" in a normal stance.

Tail: Should be set moderately high just below top line, covered with long, profuse hair and carried over back, not necessarily centered, when alert and when moving. Sometimes dropped when at rest. Tail bone should come back to hock when down. Tightly curled or double hook is a fault.

Coat: The body should be covered with soft, thick, short undercoat, with a longer, guard hair growing through it forming the outer coat, and should be free from any curl and wave. There should be a noticeably thicker mane covering the neck area, forming the ruff. Length of the outer coat will differ from dog to dog. Quality is more important than quantity.

Color: Most desirable is pure white. Permissible are white with biscuit cream, or cream.

Movement: The American Eskimo should trot, not pace. They should have a quick, agile stride that is well timed. The gait should be free, balanced, and vigorous, with good reach in the forequarters and good driving power in the hindquarters; when trotting there should be a strong rear action drive. Moving at a walk or slow trot they will not single track, or brush, but as speed increases the legs gradually angle inward until the pads are finally falling on a line directly under the longitudinal center of the body. The back should remain strong, firm, and level.

Disposition: Intelligent, alert and energetic, loyal, friendly but conservative; overly aggressive and overly shy dogs should be penalized.

Size: Miniatures: Males 12 inches up to and including 15 inches. Females 11 inches up to and including 14 inches. Puppy class only minimum height could be male 11inches and female 10 inches. Standard: males over 15 inches and up to and including 19 inches. Females over 14 inches and up to and including 18 inches.

Championship points earned as a Miniature can be carried on as a Standard.

Faults: Flop ears, pink or white eye rims, pink nose, pink lips, overshot or undershot bite, roachback, camel back, razorback, straight stifles, cowhocks, splayfeet, double curl in tail, tightly curled tail, curly coat, stilted gait, crabbing, cross over in front, hackney action.

The happy and alert expression of an American Eskimo Dog has led many to remark that it seems as if this gregarious breed is always smiling!

Disqualifications: Any color other than white, biscuit, or cream. Blue eyes. Any alterations of dog. Viciousness. Dogs that are cryptorchid or monorchid, deaf, or blind.

AN OVERVIEW OF THE AMERICAN ESKIMO STANDARDS

While the AKC and UKC breed standards do differ slightly, what they both attempt to describe is basically the same. The American Eskimo Dog is, and must always remain, a serviceable and healthy dog, free of exaggerations of any kind and ideally suited to life as a companion.

Like his undomesticated ancestors, the American Eskimo Dog retains those characteristics that would conceivably allow him to survive in the wild should the need arise. The breed has no gross exaggerations or incapacitating anatomical characteristics.

There are three separate size divisions of the American Eskimo Dog: Toy, Miniature, and Standard. The Miniature stands between 12 and 15 inches high.

The proper coat of the Eskie protects the breed from the sub-zero temperatures of winter and the scalding temperatures of summer. The longer, coarse outercoat helps shed both rain and snow while the short, dense undercoat insulates against heat and cold. The coat is especially abundant around the neck and chest, thereby offering double protection for the vital organs. Plumed tails could cover and protect the nose and mouth should the Eskie be forced to sleep in the snow. The coat should be white, but shadings of biscuit and cream are allowed. No other color is permitted.

The Eskie's balanced construction makes him an all-around canine athlete, both powerful and agile. The well-conditioned Eskie is muscular and fit with little excess to hinder his quick and easy movement. The breed is slender enough to manipulate over, under, around, and through anything. The

A well-bred American Eskimo Dog can be anything you desire— a champion, a companion, a therapy dog, and more—but definitely a best friend! Jaybar Circle B's Hide 'N' Go Seek owned by Jaqueline Brothers and Barbara Blackwood.

Eskie's length of leg keeps his vital organs well above the snow line. Small prick ears are not easily frostbitten or frozen. The muzzle has sufficient length to warm the frigid air before it reaches the lungs. The tail is carried over the back rather than trailing behind in the snow, therefore never risking the danger of being caught up in brambles or undergrowth.

What the standards ask for in the way of construction and balance applies to all three Varieties of the breed—Toy, Miniature, and Standard. While the American Eskimo Toy and Miniature Varieties may never be asked to survive in the wild, it is important to remember that they are simply a miniaturization of the Standard Variety—they are no less hardy than their larger counterpart and all aspects of type, balance, and soundness apply.

Finally, the one major difference between the two standards should be brought forth. The United Kennel Club standard does not recognize the Toy version of the American Eskimo dog as legitimate. Therefore, the Toy is not eligible to compete in UKC sanctioned events.

SELECTING the Right Eskie for You

The American Eskimo puppy you bring into your home will be your best friend and a member of your family for many years to come. Many well-bred and well-cared-for Eskies live to be 12, 15, or even 17 years of age. Therefore, it is of the utmost importance that the Eskie you select has had every opportunity to begin life in a healthy stable environment and comes from stock that is both physically and temperamentally sound.

The only way you can be ensured of this is to go directly to a breeder of

Be sure to do your homework and learn all you can about the breed before making the decision to bring an American Eskimo Dog into your family.

Playfulness and activity are often signs of a healthy and well-adjusted puppy.

American Eskimos who has consistently produced dogs of this kind over the years. A breeder earns this reputation through a well-planned breeding program that has been governed by rigid selectivity. Selective breeding programs are aimed at maintaining the breed's many fine qualities and keeping the breed free of as many genetic weaknesses as possible.

Anyone who has ever bred dogs will quickly tell you this process is both time consuming and costly for a breeder and that many never make money breeding dogs. One of the many things it does accomplish, however, is to ensure you of a dog that will be a joy to own. Responsible Eskie breeders protect their tremendous investment of time and money by basing their breeding programs on the healthiest, most representative breeding stock available. These breeders provide each following generation with the very best care and nutrition available.

Governing kennel clubs in the different countries of the world maintain lists of local breed clubs and breeders that can

lead a prospective American Eskimo Dog buyer to responsible breeders of quality stock. If you are not sure of where to contact an established Eskie breeder in your area, we strongly recommend contracting your kennel club for recommendations.

Some well-intentioned and reputable pet shop owners offer purebred puppies for sale. It should be understood, however, that in most cases the dogs offered by these shops come from distant kennels and the pet shop simply acts as the "middle man." The pet shop owner seldom has any real knowledge of the puppy's background or what kind of care he received in the critical period from birth until the time he arrived at the shop. Other pet shops carry lists of local, responsible breeders that they can send you to.

He may be tiny now, but an American Eskimo puppy will attain most of his adult size by six months of age.

There is little doubt that you will be able to find an established Eskie breeder in your own area. Finding a local breeder will allow you to visit the breeder's home or kennel, inspect the facility, and possibly see a puppy's parents and other relatives. Good breeders are always willing and able to discuss any problems that might exist in the breed and how they should be dealt with. If there aren't any Eskie breeders in your immediate area you can arrange to have a puppy shipped to you. Many breeders have shipped puppies to satisfied owners out of state and even to other countries.

Never hesitate to ask the breeder you visit or deal with by phone or mail any questions or concerns you might have relative to Eskie ownership. Expect the breeder to ask you a good number of questions as well. Good breeders are just as interested in placing their puppies in a loving and safe environment as you are in obtaining a happy healthy puppy. Most breeders will want to know if there are young children in your family

The American Eskimo puppy you choose should be bright-eyed, healthy, and interested in the world around him.

41

and what ages they are. It helps a breeder to know if you have ever owned a dog before. A concerned breeder will also want to know if you have a fenced yard and if there will be someone home during the day to attend to your young puppy's needs.

Not all good breeders maintain large kennels. In fact, you are more apt to find that Eskies come from the homes of small hobby breeders who keep only a few dogs and have litters only occasionally. The names of these people are just as likely to appear on the recommended lists from kennel clubs as the larger kennels that maintain many dogs. Hobby breeders are equally dedicated to breeding quality American Eskimos and have the advantage of being able to raise their puppies in a home environment with all the accompanying personal attention and socialization.

When searching for an American Eskimo puppy, do as much research as possible and avoid making a hasty decision. Sharon Shroeder's Pinebrook Walker's Windsong and Windstar pose for a lovely portrait.

Again, please remember it is important that both the buyer and the seller ask questions. There is no such thing as being too well informed or too inquisitive about your new acquisition. Buying an Eskie puppy is a large responsibility as well as a big undertaking. Always be suspicious of anyone who is willing to sell you an Eskie puppy with no questions asked.

RECOGNIZING A HEALTHY PUPPY

American Eskimo breeders seldom release their puppies until they are at least eight weeks of age and have been given all of their puppy vaccinations. By the time the litter is eight weeks of age they are entirely weaned or no longer nursing. While puppies are nursing they receive complete immunity from disease through their mother. Once they have stopped

Upon selection of your American Eskimo puppy, the breeder should offer a guarantee against inherited disorders.

nursing, however, they become highly susceptible to many infectious diseases. A number of these diseases can be transmitted on the hands and clothing of humans. Therefore, it is extremely important that all of your puppy's vaccinations are kept current.

A healthy Eskie puppy is a bouncy playful extrovert. Never select a puppy that appears shy or listless because you feel sorry for him. Doing so will undoubtedly lead to heartache and expensive veterinary costs. Do not attempt to make up for what the breeder did not or could not do. These efforts seldom work.

If at all possible, take the Eskie puppy of your choice into a different room in the kennel or house in which he was raised. The smells will remain the same for the puppy so he should still feel secure, but it will give you an opportunity to see how the puppy acts away from his littermates and it will give you an opportunity to inspect the puppy more closely.

Even though American Eskimo puppies are quite small (particularly those of the Toy and Miniature variety) they should feel sturdy to the touch. Puppies should not feel bony nor should their abdomens be bloated and extended. A puppy that has just eaten may have a belly that is full but the puppy should never appear obese.

A healthy puppy's ears will be pink and clean. Dark discharge or a bad odor could indicate ear mites, a sure sign of poor keeping and maintenance. An Eskie puppy's breath should always smell sweet. His teeth must be clean and bright and there should never be a malformation of the jaw, lips, or nostrils.

The puppy's eyes should be dark and clear—little spots of charcoal on a snow white background. Runny eyes or eyes that appear red and irritated could be caused by a myriad of problems, none of which indicate a healthy puppy. Coughing or diarrhea are danger signals, as is any discharge from the nose or eruptions on the skin. The coat should be soft, clean, and lustrous.

Sound conformation can be determined even at eight or ten weeks of age. The puppy's legs should be straight without bumps or malformations. The toes should point straight ahead. The back should be strong and straight and the tail carried over the back.

The puppy's attitude tells you a great deal about his health. Puppies that are feeling poorly do not react very quickly, will usually want to find a warm littermate to snuggle up to, and they will prefer to stay that way even when the rest of the gang wants to play or go exploring. The Eskie is an extrovert. Do not settle for anything less in selecting your puppy.

SIZE MATTERS

The American Eskimo Dog is bred in three sizes: Toy, Miniature, and Standard. The conformation requirements for all three varieties are exactly the same, only the size differences distinguish the varieties. Which size is best for the prospective owner depends entirely upon the personal preferences and circumstances of the owner. Needless to say,

One of the wonderful aspects of the American Eskimo Dog is that they are bred in three sizes— Toy, Miniature, and Standard—a size to fit any lifestyle!

A healthy American Eskimo puppy should have bright eyes and a shiny coat.

an eight-week-old Toy or Miniature puppy is not something that should be put into the hands of a very young child who is unaccustomed to dealing with something so fragile. Nor would an untrained and rambunctious half-grown Standard male be the right companion for an unsteady toddler. Discretion must be used in the selection of the right size Eskie for you and your family. Discussing your circumstances with a good breeder is strongly advised.

The Miniature and Toy varieties of some American Eskimo bloodlines produce individuals that may take a bit more work to keep socialized and friendly. But here again, the well-socialized puppy is the result of the owner's care and dedication.

It should be remembered that no breeder can absolutely guarantee the mature size of an American Eskimo purchased as a very young puppy. Some breeders are better able to predict size because they have a long established line made up almost exclusively of individuals of a particular size.

MALE OR FEMALE?

In many breeds, the sex of a dog in is an important consideration. There are sex-related differences in the American Eskimo that the prospective buyer should consider. In the end, however, the assets and liabilities of each sex balance each other out, and the final decision should really be based on the individual owner's preference.

The male Eskie makes just as loving, devoted, and trainable companion as the female, but in some cases he can be a bit more headstrong as an adolescent. The owner's dedication to establishing and maintaining discipline will determine the final outcome.

There is one important point to consider in choosing between a male and female dog. While both must be trained not to relieve themselves in the home, the male has a natural instinct to lift his leg and urinate to "mark" his home territory. This may be confusing to many dog owners, but a male's marking his home turf has absolutely nothing to do with whether or not the dog is housebroken. Some dogs are more difficult to train not to mark within the confines of the household than others. Males that are put out to stud are more prone to this habit than neutered males. On the other hand, females have their semi-annual heat cycles once they have reached sexual maturity. In the case of the female American Eskimo, this occurs for the first time at about six to nine months of age. These cycles are accompanied by a bloody vaginal discharge. During this time a female Eskie will need to be confined so that she does not become impregnated by neighborhood dogs and so that she does not soil her surroundings. It must be understood that the female has no control over this bloody discharge and that it cannot be controlled through training.

Both of the problems described above will not occur in dogs that are spayed or neutered. Unless an Eskie is purchased with an express agreement that they are to be used for breeding or showing, your pet should be sexually altered. Breeding and raising puppies should be left in the hands of people who have the facilities to keep each and every puppy they breed until the proper home is found for them. This can often take many months after a litter is born. Most single dog owners are not equipped for this kind of responsibility and long-term commitment. Naturally, a responsible dog owner would never allow his or her pet to roam the streets and end his life in an animal shelter. Unfortunately, being forced to place a puppy due to space or time constraints, before you are able to thoroughly check out the prospective buyer, may in fact create this exact situation. I have also heard parents inquire about buying a female dog just as a pet but with full intentions of breeding so that their children can witness "the miracle of birth." There are countless books and videos now available that portray this wonderful event and do not add to the worldwide pet overpopulation we now face.

It should be understood, however, that spaying and neutering are not reversible procedures. Spayed females or neutered males cannot be shown in conformation shows in most countries, nor can altered animals ever be used for breeding.

Choosing a male or female dog is a matter of preference, either sex will make a wonderful companion. This holiday trio of Krystal Kennel's pups surely agrees!

Another difference between the male and female Eskie concerns the coat type. There is a difference in the amount of coat carried by the male and female. The male Eskie normally carries a much heavier coat than the

female so there is more shedding during the annual springtime coat casting. However the semi-annual heat cycles of the female are also accompanied by shedding of the coat. So, while the female sheds a bit less hair, it happens twice as often.

SELECTING A SHOW-PROSPECT PUPPY

If you or your family are considering a show career for your puppy we strongly advise putting yourself in the hands of an established breeder who has earned a reputation for breeding winning show dogs. They are most capable of anticipating what one might expect a young puppy of their line to develop into when he reaches maturity.

Although the potential buyer should read the official standard of perfection for the American Eskimo, it is hard for the novice to really understand the nuances of what is being asked for. The experienced breeder is best equipped to do so and will be only too happy to assist you in your quest. However, it is important to remember that no one can make accurate predictions or guarantees on a very young puppy.

Any predictions a breeder makes are based upon their experience with past litters that produced winning show dogs. It should be obvious that the more successful a breeder has been in producing winning Eskies through the years, the broader his or her basis of comparison will be.

The most any responsible breeder will say about an eight-week-old puppy is that he has "show potential." If you are serious about showing your Eskie, most breeders strongly suggest waiting until a puppy is at least four or five months old before making any decisions.

A reputable breeder will be able to tell you if the pup you are considering has "show potential."

There are many shortcomings an American Eskimo puppy might have that would in no way interfere with him being a wonderful companion but could be serious drawbacks in the show ring. However, a beginning breed fancier may not be able to identify these things. This is why employing the assistance of a good breeder is so important. Still, the prospective buyer should be at least generally aware of what the Eskie show puppy should

Your Eskie puppy will look to you, his owner, to provide for all his needs. Before purchasing a puppy, many breeders require you to sign a contract ensuring particular aspects of his care and maintenance.

American Eskimo puppies are social creatures and need the company of other Eskies when young. The more time your Eskie spends with other animals, the better socialized he will become.

look like and know what faults constitute disqualifications according to the standard and would preclude them from competing in AKC or UKC conformation shows.

The show-prospect puppy must have a happy outgoing temperament. He will be

a compact little bundle of fluff, never appearing short-legged or out of balance. The show puppy should move around with ease, his head held high, and his tail carried over his back. Dark eyes, black nose, black lips, and black eye rims are all required. The Eskimo Dog's ears are usually held erect by eight weeks of age. Be sure to examine the ear leather for any signs of weakness.

The only allowable colors for an Eskie are white, biscuit, and cream. Though a pure white coat is preferred, many puppies have shadings of cream on the head. In most cases this color disappears entirely by the time the puppy has achieved adulthood. The breeder from whom you purchase your Eskie will be able to tell you what to expect in regard to your puppy's coat color.

PUPPY OR ADULT?

For the person anticipating a show career for their Eskie or for someone hoping to become a breeder, the purchase of a young adult provides greater certainty with respect to quality. Even those who simply want a companion could consider the adult dog.

In some instances, breeders will have males or females they no longer wish to use for breeding. After the dogs have been altered they would prefer to have them live out their lives in a

Like mother, like daughter! Often the temperament of a puppy will be much like her parents.

private home with plenty of care and attention. Acquiring an adult dog eliminates the many problems raising a puppy involves, and Eskies are a breed that "transfer" well, provided they are given the affection and attention they need.

Depending upon your family's lifestyle, adopting an older dog may be the right decision for you.

Elderly people often prefer an adult dog, particularly one that is housebroken. The adult dog can be easier to manage because it requires less supervision and damage control. Adult Eskies are seldom "chewers" and are usually more than ready to adapt to household rules.

However, there are concerns involved with acquiring an adult dog. Adult dogs have usually developed behaviors that may or may not fit into your routine. If an adult Eskie has never been exposed to small children, the dog may be totally perplexed, often frightened, by this new experience. We strongly advise taking an adult dog into your home on a trial basis to see if the dog will adapt to your lifestyle and environment. Most often the transition is successful, but on rare occasions a prospective owner decides they would prefer to train their dog from puppyhood.

IDENTIFICATION PAPERS

The purchase of any purebred dog entitles you to three very important documents: a health record including a list of inoculations, a copy of the dog's pedigree, and a registration certificate.

You will find that most American Eskimo breeders have initiated the necessary preliminary inoculation series for their puppies by the time they are eight weeks of age. These inoculations temporarily protect the puppies against hepatitis, leptospirosis, distemper, and canine parvovirus. Permanent vaccinations should follow at a time prescribed by your veterinarian. Since breeders and veterinarians follow different approaches to inoculations, it is important that the health record you obtain for your puppy accurately lists which shots have been given and when. This way the veterinarian you choose will be able to continue with the appropriate inoculation series as needed. In most cases rabies inoculations are not given until a puppy is six months of age or older.

A pedigree is your dog's "family tree." The breeder must supply you with a copy of this document authenticating your puppy's ancestors back to at least the third generation. In this way, you will be able to prove, beyond a shadow of a doubt, that your American Eskimo is pure bred.

A registration certificate is the canine world's "birth certificate." The governing kennel club in the country of your puppy's birth issues this certificate. When you transfer the ownership of your Eskie from the breeder's name to your own name, the transaction is entered on this certificate and then mailed to the appropriate kennel club, where it is permanently recorded in their files.

Keep all of your dog's documents in a safe place, you will need them when you visit your veterinarian or if you should ever wish to breed or show your Eskie. Keep

A pedigree will prove that the parents of your puppy were purebred American Eskimo Dogs.

the name, address, and phone number of the breeder from whom you purchase your dog as well. Should you ever lose any of these important documents, you will then be able to contact the breeder regarding duplicates.

Diet Sheet

Your Eskie is the happy healthy puppy he is because the breeder has been carefully feeding and caring for him. Every breeder has their own particular way of doing things. Most breeders give new owners a written record that details the amount and kind of food a puppy has been receiving. Follow these recommendations to the letter, at least for the first month or two after the puppy comes to live with you.

Looks like this guy can't get enough to eat! It is important to provide your Eskie with a diet that meets his nutritional needs.

The diet sheet should indicate the number of times a day your puppy is accustomed to being fed and the kind of vitamin supplementation he has been receiving. Following the prescribed procedure will reduce the chance of upset stomach and loose stools.

A breeder's diet sheet usually projects the increases and changes in food that will be necessary as your puppy grows from week to week. If the sheet does not include this information, ask the breeder for suggestions regarding increases and the eventual changeover to adult food.

In the unlikely event you are not supplied with a diet sheet by the breeder and are unable to get one, your veterinarian will be able to advise you in this respect. There are countless foods now being manufactured expressly to meet the nutritional needs of puppies and growing dogs. A trip down the pet aisle at your supermarket will prove just how many choices you have. Two important tips to remember: read labels carefully for content, and you very often get what you pay for.

Health Guarantee

Any reputable breeder is more than willing to supply a written agreement that the purchase of your Eskie is contingent upon his passing a veterinarian's examination.

Ideally, you will be able to arrange an appointment with your chosen veterinarian right after you have picked up your puppy from the breeder and before you take the puppy home. If this is not possible, you should not delay this procedure any longer than 72 hours from the time you take your puppy home.

TEMPERAMENT AND SOCIALIZATION

Temperament is both hereditary and learned. Poor treatment and lack of proper socialization can ruin inherited good temperament. An American Eskimo puppy that comes from shy or nervous stock or already exhibits these characteristics himself will make a poor companion or show dog and should certainly never be bred. Therefore, it is critical that you obtain a happy puppy from a breeder who is determined to produce good temperament and has taken all the necessary steps early on to provide the proper socialization.

Temperaments in the same litter can range from confident and outgoing to shy and fearful, but by and large the American Eskimo temperament is and should be confident. This attitude is a hallmark of the breed. Although any dog will prefer his family to strangers, it is your responsibility to keep your Eskie well socialized.

If you are fortunate enough to have children in the household or living nearby, the task of socializing your puppy will be assisted considerably. Eskies raised with children often have the best dispositions. The two seem to understand each other and, in some way known only to the puppies and children themselves, they give each other the confidence to face the trying ordeal of growing up.

The children in your own household are not the only children your American Eskimo should spend time with. It is a case of the more the merrier! Every child (and adult for that matter) that enters your household should be introduced to your Eskie. Your puppy should go everywhere with you: the post office, market, even to the shopping mall. Be prepared to create a stir wherever you go—the very reason that attracted you to the first Eskie you met applies other people as well. Everyone will want to pet your little ball of fluff and there is nothing in the world that will make socialization easier.

Should your puppy recoil from a stranger, pick him up and hand him to the person. The young Eskie will quickly learn that all humans are friends. Remember, you are in charge and must call the shots.

If your Eskie has a show career in his future, there are other things in addition to just being handled that he will have to be taught. All American Eskimo show dogs must learn to have their mouths inspected by the judge. Males must be accustomed to having their testicles touched so the judge can determine that all male dogs are "complete"(that there are two normal sized testicles in the scrotum.) These inspections must begin in puppyhood and be done on a regular and continuing basis.

A properly socialized American Eskimo Dog will be a peaceful member of your household, able to get along with all the other animals in residence.

Eskies should be entirely compatible with other dogs as well as with humans. If you are fortunate enough to have a dog park nearby, visit it with your puppy as frequently as possible. A young Eskie that has been exposed regularly to other dogs from puppyhood will learn to accept other dogs and other breeds much more readily than an Eskie that seldom ever sees other dogs.

THE ADOLESCENT AMERICAN ESKIMO DOG

Although Eskies have usually attained their full height by 11 or 12 months of age, they are far from mature. Some lines achieve maturity at around two years of age. Others are almost three before they are fully developed.

At about six to nine months the adult coat has begun to replace the puppy fuzz. You will notice a change in hair texture as well. The new hair that comes in will be much coarser. Up until this time the puppy coat is relatively easy to care for. Thorough brushing will only take a few minutes two or three times a week. It is important, however, that you

attend to these grooming sessions regularly during the early months of your Eskie's growth. The coat change period will require more of your time because the dead puppy hair is loosening and being replaced by new adult hair. Mats occur easily and frequently during this time. If your Eskie has been groomed regularly, you will find your task much easier.

Your Eskie's dietary needs change during this growth period. Some Eskies seem as if they can never get enough to eat, while others eat just enough to avoid starving. Think of Eskie puppies as individuals and act accordingly. The amount of food you give your Eskie should be adjusted according to how much he will readily consume at each meal. If the entire meal is eaten quickly, add a small amount to the next feeding and continue to do so as the need increases. This method will ensure that you give your puppy enough food. But pay close attention to the dog's appearance and condition because you do not want a puppy to become overweight or obese.

Your Eskie will soon "grow into" an adult diet, but during his first few weeks at your home, stick to your breeder's recommendation.

At eight weeks of age an Eskie puppy should be eating four meals a day. By the time he is six months old, the puppy can do well on two meals a day, perhaps with a snack in the middle of the day. If your puppy does not eat the food offered, he is either not hungry or not well. Your dog will eat when he is hungry. If you suspect your dog is not well, a trip to the veterinarian is in order.

The adolescent period is a particularly important one. It is during this time that your American Eskimo must learn all the household and social rules by which he will live for the rest of his life. Your patience and commitment during this time will not only produce a respected canine good citizen but will forge a bond between the two of you that will grow and ripen into a wonderful relationship.

A well-socialized American Eskimo Dog will be a lifelong, loyal companion. UKC Grand Ch. Winterset Sweetie Pie, owned by Donna R. Hays, serves as a pillow for her sleepy mistress.

CARING for Your American Eskimo Dog

FEEDING AND NUTRITION

The best way to make sure your Eskie puppy is obtaining the right amount and type of food for his age is to follow the diet sheet provided by your breeder. Do your best not to change the puppy's diet and you will be less apt to run into digestive problems. Problems like diarrhea can cause rapid dehydration and severe consequences.

If it is necessary to change your Eskie puppy's diet for any reason it should be done gradually, over a period of several meals and a few days. Begin by adding a tablespoon or two of the new food, gradually increasing the amount until the meal consists entirely of the new product.

By the time your Eskie is 10 to 12 months old you can reduce feedings to once a day. This meal can be given either in the morning or evening. It is really a matter of choice on your part. There are two important things to remember: feed the main meal at the same time every day and make sure the food you feed is nutritionally complete.

The single meal can be supplemented by a snack of hard dog biscuits made especially for smaller dogs. These biscuits not only become highly anticipated treats, but also are genuinely helpful in maintaining healthy gums and teeth.

A healthy American Eskimo Dog will look forward to mealtime! Looks like this Eskie enjoyed his supper.

Balanced Diets

In order for a canine diet to qualify as complete and balanced in the United States, it must meet standards set by the Subcommittee on Canine Nutrition of the National Research Council of the National Academy of Sciences. Most commercial foods manufactured for dogs meet these standards and prove

Consult your breeder or veterinarian about the appropriate diet for your American Eskimo Dog.

Puppies grow very quickly and require especially nutritious meals to grow into healthy adults.

this by listing the ingredients contained in the food on every package or can.

The ingredients are listed in descending order with the main ingredient listed first.

Fed with any regularity at all, refined sugars can cause your Eskie to become obese and will definitely create tooth decay. Canine teeth are not genetically disposed to handling sugars. Do not feed your Eskie candy or sweets and avoid products that contain sugar in any high degree.

Fresh water and a properly prepared, balanced diet containing the essential nutrients in the correct proportions are all a healthy American Eskimo Dog needs to be offered. Dog foods are prepared in a variety of ways. There are moist canned foods, dry kibble, and semi-moist chunks. Many dog foods claim to be "scientifically fortified" and "all-natural."

This little Eskie knows the place to be at dinner time— under the family dinner table!

It is important to remember that all dogs, whether they are Chihuahuas, American Eskimos, or Great Danes, are carnivorous (meat-eating) animals. While the vegetable content of your Eskie's diet should not be overlooked, a dog's physiology and anatomy is based upon carnivorous food

acquisition. Protein and fat are absolutely essential to the well-being of your dog. In fact, it is wise to add a small amount of vegetable oil or bacon fat to your dog's meals, particularly during the winter months, to help him meet these requirements. Always read the list of ingredients on the dog food you buy. Animal protein should appear first on the label's list. If you are feeding quality kibble, add meat and some healthy table scraps to provide a nutritious meal for your Eskie.

Please realize that carnivores in the wild eat the entire beast they capture and kill. The carnivore's kill will almost always be

There are a number of quality dog foods and treats available that will offer special nutritional value to your growing pup.

a herbivore (plant-eating animal). Invariably, the carnivore begins his meal with the contents of the herbivore's stomach. This provides the carbohydrates, minerals, and nutrients present in vegetables. Our dogs are entirely dependent upon us for their well-being. Therefore, we are responsible for duplicating the food balance the wild dog finds in nature. The domesticated dog's diet must include protein, carbohydrates, fats, roughage, and small amounts of essential minerals and vitamins.

Finding commercially prepared diets that contain all the necessary nutrients your Eskie needs should not present a problem. Be sure to understand exactly what the diet you have chosen for your Eskie provides for him. Many commercially prepared foods already contain all the necessary components your Eskie needs for a well-balanced diet. Consult your veterinarian and breeder about extra vitamin supplementation.

Oversupplementation

A great deal of controversy exists today regarding the orthopedic problems, such as hip and patella (knee) dysplasia, that afflict many breeds. Some claim these problems are entirely hereditary, many others feel they are exacerbated by the use of mineral and vitamin supplements in young puppies.

Vitamin supplementation is not an exact science. You should *never* exceed the amount your veterinarian prescribes to your Eskie, and even then many Eskie breeders insist that all recommended dosages be halved before including them in a dog's diet. Other breeders feel no supplementation should be given at all, believing a balanced diet that includes animal protein, milk products, some fat, and a small amount of bone meal are all that is necessary for your Eskies healthy life. Pregnant and lactating bitches may require supplementation of some kind, but extreme caution is advised and dosages should always be discussed with your veterinarian.

If the owner of an American Eskimo normally eats healthy nutritious food, there is no reason why their dog cannot be given table scraps. Table scraps should be given only as part of the dog's meal and never from the table. An Eskie that becomes accustomed to being hand fed from the table can become a real pest at meal time. Also dinner guests may find the pleading stare of your Eskie less than appealing when dinner is being served.

Dogs do not care if their food looks like a hot dog or a piece of cheese. Truly nutritious dog foods are seldom manufactured to look like food that appeals to humans. Dogs only care about how food smells and tastes. It is highly doubtful you will be eating your dog's food so do not waste your money on these products. Also, most of the moist or canned foods that have the look of "delicious red beef" look that way because they contain large amounts of red dye. These should not be fed to any dog! The same coloring that makes these products look red is so strong it can actually stain and discolor your Eskie's coat. Some breeders of white dogs claim these products cause tearing that stains your Eskie's face and detracts from the breed's beautiful expression.

To test the dye content of either canned or dry foods, place a small amount of the food on an absorbent towel after it has been moistened or prepared. Allow the food to remain there for several hours. If the paper is stained, the dye content is too high and you will risk staining your Eskie's beautiful white coat.

Special Diets

There are many commercially prepared diets for dogs that have special dietary needs. There are special foods on the market made especially for the overweight, underweight, or geriatric dog. The calorie content of these foods is adjusted according to the requirements of the individuals to whom they are catering. With the correct amount of the right foods and the proper amount of exercise, your Eskie should stay in top shape. Again, common sense must prevail. Too many calories will increase weight, cutting back on calories will reduce weight.

Occasionally, a young Eskie going through the teething period or a female coming into season will stop eating their food. The concerned owner's first response is often to tempt the dog by hand feeding special treats and foods that the problem eater

It seems that "Jake" of Gordon Patterson's household prefers red wine and the evening paper served with his dinner!

The American Eskimo Dog is active and energetic and will benefit greatly from plenty of time outdoors. Jay Bar Circle B Phoebe's Katidid, owned by Jaqueline Brothers and Barbara Blackwood, takes a break to stop and smell the tulips.

seems to prefer. This practice only serves to compound the problem. Once a dog learns to play the waiting game, he will turn up his nose at anything other than his favorite food, knowing full well what he wants to eat will eventually arrive.

Unlike humans, dogs have no suicidal tendencies. A healthy dog will not starve himself to death. He may not eat enough to keep himself in the shape we find ideal and attractive, but he will definitely eat enough to maintain himself. If your Eskie is not eating properly and appears to be too thin, it is probably best to consult your veterinarian.

SPECIAL NEEDS OF THE AMERICAN ESKIMO DOG

Exercise

Within reason, most anything you can do, your Eskie can do. Long morning walks, hikes over mountain trails, exploring tide pools along the beach—your Eskie will enjoy and benefit from these activities as much as you will.

On the other hand, if your idea of exercise is closer to a walk around the block than to a marathon, your Eskie can be just as satisfied. The American Eskimo is not a breed that requires taking your energy level to its outer limits. In fact, if your Eskie shares his life with young children or other dogs he could easily be getting all the exercise he needs to stay fit. The Eskie is always ready for a romp or to invent some new game that entails plenty of aerobic activity. Slow steady exercise that keeps your companion's heart rate in the working area will only help to extend his life. If your Eskie is doing all this with you at his side, you are increasing the chances that the two of you will enjoy each other's company for many more years to come.

The Eskie is by nature a happy dog that enjoys the company of others. On a warm day "Jake" and Gordon enjoy a swim.

Naturally, common sense must be used in regard to the extent and intensity of the exercise you give your American Eskimo. Remember that young puppies have short bursts of energy and then require long rest periods. No puppy of any breed should be forced to

accompany you on extended runs—serious injuries can result. Most adult Eskies will willingly walk as far, perhaps further, than their owners are inclined to go. Daily walks combined with some game playing in the yard can keep the average Eskie in fine shape.

Hot Weather

Special precautions must be taken when your Eskie exercises in hot weather. Plan your walks for the first thing in the morning if at all possible. If you cannot arrange to do this, wait until the sun has set and the outdoor temperature has dropped to a comfortable degree.

No dog should ever be left in a car in hot weather. Temperatures can soar in a matter of minutes and your dog can die of heat exhaustion in less time than you would ever imagine. Rolling down the windows helps little and is dangerous in that an overheated dog will panic and attempt to escape through an open window. A word to the wise–leave your Eskie at home in a cool room on hot days.

Cold weather, even temperatures hovering around the zero mark, are no problem at all for the American Eskimo. The only

The Kerrys proudly display the new addition to their family, Karuk's Bit of Silver.

warm clothing required for your winter walks will be yours, as long as the two of you keep moving. However, do not allow your Eskie to remain wet if the two of you get caught in the rain. At the very least, thoroughly towel dry the wet Eskie to prevent him from catching a cold.

Socialization

The same qualities that make the American Eskimo such a fine guardian and watchdog create a tendency in the breed to be aloof and a trifle wary when it comes to strangers. While this is certainly not a fault, without proper socialization the Eskie can become extremely shy and introverted.

It is important to remember that an Eskie puppy may be happy as a clam living at home with you and your family, but if the socialization begun by the breeder is not continued, that sunny disposition will not extend outside your front door. From the day the young Eskie arrives in your home you must

be committed to providing him with various opportunities for exploration and inspection of the world around him.

If you introduce your Eskies to children while they are still young, they will make friends that last a lifetime.

GROOMING Your American Eskimo Dog

It is important to remember that the American Eskimo Dog requires nearly no clipping or trimming. Breeders are adamant that Eskie lovers not fall into grooming fads of any kind. Proper brushing is all the grooming that your Eskie will ever need unless he is destined for the show ring. With patience both you and your Eskie will come to enjoy the time spent on grooming.

PUPPY COAT

Undoubtedly, the breeder from whom you purchased your Eskie puppy will have started to accustom your puppy to

Before you begin trimming of any kind, you must brush your Eskie's coat thoroughly to be sure it is mat free.

grooming just as soon as there was enough hair to brush. You must continue with grooming sessions or begin them at once if they have not been started. You and your Eskie will spend many hours involved in this activity over the years. If you both learn to cooperate, grooming will be an easy and pleasant experience.

The first piece of equipment you will have to purchase is a grooming table. Make sure the table is of a height that allows you to work comfortably while you are sitting or standing. Adjustable-height grooming tables are available at most pet shops. Although you will buy one when your Eskie puppy first arrives, anticipate your dog's full-grown size in making your purchase and select a table that will accommodate a fully grown Eskie lying on his side.

You will also need to invest in two brushes, a steel comb, barber's scissors, a pair of nail clippers, commercial coat conditioner, and a spray bottle. Consider the fact you will be using this equipment for many years so buy the best of these items that you can afford.

Do not attempt to groom your Eskie on the floor. A puppy will only attempt to get away from you when he has decided enough is enough, and you will spend a good part of your time chasing the puppy around the room.

The Eskie puppy should be taught to lie on his side to be groomed. He should be kept in that position for most of the

grooming process. The puppy will also have to be kept in the sitting and standing position, but the lying position takes the most time and is more difficult for the puppy to learn. The Eskie trained to lie quietly on his side will prove to be a true godsend when the dog is fully grown and has developed a mature coat.

Begin this training by picking the puppy up with his side against your chest and your arms wrapped around the puppy's body. Lay the puppy down on the table, release your arms, but keep your chest pressed lightly down on the puppy's side. Speak reassuringly to the puppy, stroking his head and rump. Do this a number of times before you attempt to do any grooming. Repeat the process until your puppy understands what he is supposed to do when you place him on the grooming table.

All lathered up with no place to go! These American Eskimo puppies eagerly await their turn to be rinsed off.

Start with the slicker brush and begin what is called "line brushing" at the top of the shoulder to the base of the neck.

Part the hair in a straight line from the front of the shoulder straight on down to the bottom of the chest. Brush through the hair to the right and left of the part, lightly spraying the area with the coat conditioner as you go. Start at the skin and brush out to the very end of the hair. Do a small section at a time and continue on down the part. When you reach the bottom of the part return to the top and make another part just to the right of the first line you brushed. *Part, brush, and spray.* You will repeat this process, working toward the rear, until you reach the puppy's tail.

Never allow your American Eskimo Dog to remain wet after a bath. Wrap him in a clean towel and dry him thoroughly.

I prefer to do the legs on the same side I have been working on at this time. Use the same process, parting the hair at the top of the leg and working down. Do this all around the leg and be especially careful to attend to the hard-to-reach areas under the upper legs where they join the body. Mats occur in these areas very rapidly, especially during the time when the Eskie is shedding his puppy coat.

Should you encounter a mat that does not brush out easily, use your fingers and the steel comb to separate the hairs as much as possible. Do not cut or pull out the matted hair. Apply baby powder or one of the specially prepared grooming powders directly to the mat and brush completely from the skin out.

When you have finished the legs on the one side, turn the puppy over and complete the entire process on the other side—*part, spray, brush.* As your Eskie becomes accustomed to this process you may find he considers this nap time. You may have to lift your puppy into a sitting position to arouse him from his slumber.

While the puppy is sitting you can do the hair of the chest and neck. Be particularly thorough in the area right behind the ears, as it is highly mat prone. Use the line-brushing method here as well. Next, stand the puppy up and do the tail. Check the longer hair of the "pants" on the rear legs to make sure they are thoroughly brushed, especially around the area of the anus and genitalia. Needless to say, it is important to be extremely careful when brushing in these areas because they are extremely sensitive and easily injured.

Finishing Touches

When the line-brushing process is completed it is time for the finishing touches. Use your barber scissors to trim the long or shaggy hairs around your Eskie's feet. You may trim off your Eskie's whiskers if you wish. This is optional, however; many Eskie owners prefer to leave the whiskers on.

Being clean is for sissies! Helen Dick looks in amazement at what five minutes outdoors has done to her newly groomed and bathed Eskie puppy.

Brush the hair forward around the head, shoulders, and the back. Do the same with the hair of the tail. Brush the chest hair downward and do the same with the hair on the sides of the dog.

NAIL TRIMMING

During grooming you should accustom your Eskie to having his nails trimmed and his feet inspected. Always inspect your dog's feet for cracked pads. Check between the toes for splinters and thorns. Pay particular attention to any swollen or tender areas. In many sections of the country there is a weed called a "fishtail" that has a barbed hook-like affair and carries a seed. This hook easily finds its way into an Eskie's foot or between his toes and very quickly works its way deep into the dog's flesh. This will cause soreness and infection. Fishtails are best removed by your veterinarian before serious problems result.

The nails of an Eskie that spends most of his time indoors or on grass when outdoors can grow long very quickly. Do not allow the nails to become overgrown and then expect to cut

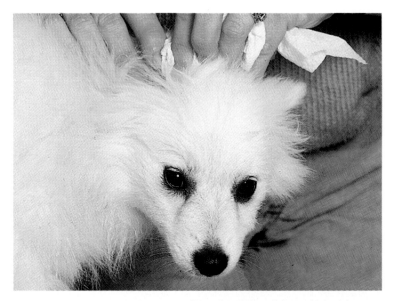

If you accustom your Eskie to grooming procedures at an early age, he will come to think of it as a pleasant experience.

them back easily. Each nail has a blood vessel running through the center called the "quick." The quick grows close to the end of the nail and contains very sensitive nerve endings. If the nail is allowed to grow too long it will be impossible to cut it back to a proper length without cutting into the quick. This causes severe pain to the dog and can also result in a great deal of bleeding that can be very difficult to stop.

If your Eskie is getting plenty of exercise on cement or rough hard pavement, the nails may keep sufficiently worn down. Otherwise, the nails can grow long very quickly. They must then be trimmed with canine nail clippers, an electric nail grinder (also called a drummel), or a coarse file made expressly for that purpose. Any of these items can be purchased at major pet emporiums.

We prefer the electric nail grinder over the others because it is so easy to control and helps avoid cutting into the quick. If your Eskie has dark nails it may be practically impossible to see where the quick ends, so regardless of which nail trimming device is used, one must proceed with caution and remove only a small portion of the nail at time.

Use of the electric grinder requires introducing your puppy to it at an early age. The instrument has a whining sound to it, not unlike a dentist's drill. The noise combined with the vibration of the sanding head on the nail itself can take some getting used to, but most dogs eventually accept it as one of life's trials. Most Eskies do not like having their nails trimmed no matter what device is used. My decision was to use the grinder because I find that I am less apt to damage the quick using this tool.

Should the quick be nipped in the trimming process, there are any number of blood-clotting products available at pet shops that will almost immediately stem the flow of blood. It is wise to have one of these products on hand in case there is a nail trimming accident or the dog tears a nail on his own.

This American Eskimo puppy looks perfectly comfortable on the grooming table while being blow-dried.

Hopefully you and your Eskie have spent the many months between puppyhood and full maturity learning to assist each other through the grooming process. The two of you have survived the shedding of the puppy coat and the arrival of the entirely different

adult hair. Not only is the Eskie's adult hair of an entirely different texture, it is much longer and much thicker.

By this time you have realized that the pin brush, with its longer bristles set in rubber, is far more effective for line brushing the adult Eskie than the slicker brush that you used through puppyhood. However, brushing the adult coat should be no different then when your Eskie was a puppy. The obvious difference is that you have more dog and more hair.

While one might expect grooming an adult Standard Eskie to be a monumental task, this is not necessarily so. The two of you have been practicing the brushing routine for so long it should be second nature by now. Additionally, the adult Eskie's hair is actually much easier to cope with than the puppy coat. Ten minutes a day with a brush, plus a thorough weekly session, will keep your Eskie looking great!

However, if the coat is neglected and becomes matted, you will indeed have a difficult time ahead of you. You may have to resort to having a veterinarian or groomer shave the matted Eskie. Resort to shaving only under extreme circumstances.

BATHING

If you groom your American Eskimo Dog regularly he will almost never require bathing. Dog show exhibitors use coat care products that adhere to the Eskie's hair and may make bathing necessary on occasion. However, even most Eskie exhibitors use "dry bath" products rather than the tub and shampoo method. Well-kept Eskies are literally odor free, and frequent bathing serves little purpose. Bathing can dry out the Eskie's skin and hair, creating unnecessary problems.

Your American Eskimo Dog will look to you, his owner, to provide for all his grooming needs.

If you must bathe your Eskie, never bathe him while he is matted. Wetting matted hair will only complicate the situation and result in much more work than

completing the mat removal process prior to bathing. On the rare occasions your Eskie requires a wet bath you will need to gather the necessary equipment ahead of time.

A rubber mat should be placed at the bottom of the tub to avoid having your Eskie slip. A rubber spray hose is necessary to thoroughly wet the dense coat. The hose also helps to remove all shampoo residue.

A small cotton ball placed inside each ear will avoid water running down into the dog's ear canal and a drop of mineral oil or a dab of petroleum jelly placed in each eye will preclude shampoo irritating the Eskie's eyes.

It is best to use a shampoo designed especially for white dogs. The pH balance is adjusted to keep drying to a minimum and leaves the hair clean, shining, and lustrous.

When bathing, start behind the ears and work back. Use a wash cloth to soap and rinse around the head and face. Once you have shampooed your Eskie you must rinse the coat thoroughly. When you feel quite certain that all shampoo residue has been removed, rinse once more. Shampoo residue in the coat is sure to dry the hair and could cause your Eskie skin irritation.

You must never ignore your Eskie's feet during grooming. Check for cracked footpads and keep his nails trimmed short to prevent injury.

As soon as you have completed the bath use heavy towels to remove as much of the excess water as possible. Your Eskie will assist you in the process by shaking a great deal of the water out of his coat on his own—beware!

Before your Eskie is completely dry, brush out his coat to keep mats and tangles from forming. Use the same brushing procedures you normally use.

My advice is to avoid a wet bath unless it is absolutely necessary. There are so many effective dry bath products available that a time-consuming wet bath is only necessary as a last resort.

HOUSEBREAKING and Training Your Eskie

There is no breed of dog that cannot be trained. It does appear that some breeds are more difficult to get the desired response from than others. In many cases, however, this has more to do with the training methods than the dog's inability to learn. With the proper approach, any dog that is not mentally deficient can be taught to be a good canine citizen. Many dog owners do not understand how a dog learns and do not realize they can be breed specific in their approach to training.

Young puppies have an amazing capacity to learn. This capacity is greater than most humans realize. It is important to remember, though, these young puppies also forget with great speed

Young Starlights AE Sings The Blues, owned by Shirley Tooker, gets ready for a game of keep-away with the car keys.

A well-trained American Eskimo Dog can do anything. Ch. Sundance's Krystal Lace and her friend Jamey set out for an evening of Halloween fun!

unless they are reminded of what they have learned by continual reinforcement.

As puppies leave the nest they begin their search for two things: a pack leader and the rules set down by that leader by which they can abide. Because puppies, particularly American Eskimo puppies, are cuddly and cute, some owners fail miserably in supplying these very basic needs. Instead, the owner immediately begins to respond to the demands of the puppy, and Eskie puppies can quickly learn to be very demanding.

For example, an Eskie puppy quickly learns he will be allowed into the house because he is barking or whining, not because he can only enter the house when he is *not* barking or whining. Instead of learning that the only way he will be fed is to follow a set procedure (i.e., sitting or lying down on command), the Eskie puppy learns that leaping about the kitchen and barking is what gets results.

If a young puppy cannot find his pack leader in an owner, the puppy himself assumes the role. If there are no rules imposed, the puppy learns to make his own. And, unfortunately, the negligent owner continually reinforces the puppy's decisions by allowing him to govern the household.

With small dogs like the Miniature or Toy varieties of the American Eskimo, this scenario can produce a neurotic nuisance. In a top-size Standard, the situation can be downright dangerous. Neither situation is an acceptable one.

The key to successful training lies in establishing the proper relationship between dog and owner. The owner or the owning family must be the pack leader and the individual or family must provide the rules by which the dog abides.

The Gumabone™, made by Nylabone®, helps control plaque, eases the need to chew, and is nutritious. It is highly recommended as a healthy toy for your Eskie.

Once leadership is established, ease of training depends in great part upon just how much a dog depends on his master's approval.

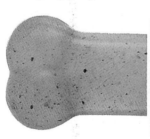

The entirely dependent dog lives to please his master and will do everything in his power to evoke the approval response from the person he is devoted to.

At the opposite end of the pole we have the totally independent dog that is not remotely concerned with what his master thinks. Dependency varies from one breed to the next and to degrees within breeds as well. Eskies are no exception to this rule. Fortunately for the owner, the average Eskie falls somewhere near the middle of the dependency spectrum, and while certainly not a "pushover," the breed is highly trainable.

HOUSEBREAKING

The Crate Method

A major key to successfully training your American Eskimo, whether it is obedience training or housebreaking, is

Your American Eskimo Dog's crate should be made into a cozy den where he can relax. Line it with a soft blanket and provide him with toys to make him feel right at home.

avoidance. It is much easier for your Eskie to learn something if you do not first have to have him unlearn some bad habit. The crate training method of housebreaking is a highly successful method of avoiding bad habits in the first place.

First-time dog owners are inclined to initially see the crate method of housebreaking as cruel, but those same people will return later and thank us profusely for having suggested it in the first place. They are also surprised to find that the puppy will eventually come to think of his crate as a place of private retreat—a den to which he will retreat for rest and privacy. The success of the crate method is based upon the fact that puppies will not soil the area in which they sleep unless they are forced to.

The use of a crate reduces housetraining time to an absolute minimum and avoids keeping a puppy under constant stress by incessantly correcting him for making mistakes in the house.

The anti-cage advocates consider it cruel to confine a puppy for any length of time but find no problem in constantly harassing and punishing the puppy because he has wet on the carpet or relieved himself behind the sofa.

Crates come in a wide variety of styles. The fiberglass shipping kennels used by many airlines are popular with many Eskie owners, but residents of the warmer climates sometimes prefer the wire type. Both are available at pet stores.

There are many sizes to choose from as well. The size you select will depend upon the anticipated size of your Eskie puppy when he is fully grown.

The crate used for housebreaking should only be large enough for the puppy to stand up, lie down, and stretch out in comfort. It is not necessary to dash out and buy a new crate every few weeks to accommodate the Eskie's rapid spurts of growth. Simply partition off the excess space in the crate and move it back as needed. Long before you have lost the need for the partition your Eskie will be housebroken.

Begin feeding your Eskie puppy in his crate. Keep the door closed and latched while the puppy is eating. When the meal is finished, open the crate and *carry* the puppy outdoors to the spot where you want him to learn to eliminate. In the event you do not have outdoor access or will be away from home for long periods of time, begin housebreaking by placing newspapers in some out of the way corner that is easily accessible for the puppy. If you consistently take your puppy to the same spot you will reinforce the habit of going there for that purpose.

It is important that you do not let the puppy loose after eating. Young puppies will eliminate almost immediately after eating or drinking. They will also be ready to relieve themselves

Eskies are naturally mischievous and playful. Early basic training will be much more successful if you make it fun and interesting.

This quartet of revelers demonstrates the ultimate in good behavior. If it weren't for basic training, that birthday cake would surely be devoured!

when they first wake up and after playing. If you keep a watchful eye on your puppy you will quickly learn when this is about to take place. A puppy usually circles and sniffs the floor just before he will relieve himself. Do not give your puppy an opportunity to learn that he can eliminate in the house! Your housetraining chores will be reduced considerably if you avoid this in the first place.

If you are not able to watch your puppy every minute, he should be in his crate with the door securely latched. Each time you put your puppy in the crate give him a small treat of some kind. Throw the treat to the back of the crate and encourage the puppy to walk in on his own. When he does so, praise him and perhaps hand him another piece of the treat through the opening in the front of the crate.

Do not succumb to your puppy's complaints about being in his crate. The Eskie puppy must learn to stay there and to do so without unnecessary complaining. A quick "no" command and a tap on the crate will usually get the puppy to understand that theatrics will not result in liberation. (Remember that you, the pack leader, make the rules and the puppy is seeking to learn what they are!)

If you allow your American Eskimo Dog to develop bad habits, like lying on the furniture, it can be very hard to break him of it later.

Understand that an Eskie puppy of 8 to 12 weeks will not be able to contain himself for long periods of time. Puppies of that age must relieve themselves every few hours except at night. Your schedule must be adjusted accordingly. Also make sure your puppy has relieved himself, both bowel and bladder, the last thing at night and do not dawdle when you wake up in the morning.

Your first priority in the morning is to get the puppy outdoors. Just how early this ritual will take place will depend much more on your puppy than on you. If your Eskie is like most others, there will be no doubt in your mind when he needs to be let out. You will also very quickly learn to tell the difference between the "this is an emergency" complaint and the "I just want out" grumbling. Do not test the young puppy's ability to contain himself. His vocal demands are confirmation that the housebreaking lesson is being learned.

Should you find it necessary to be away from home all day you will not be able to leave your puppy in a crate. Do not make the mistake of allowing him to roam the house or even a large room at will. Confine the puppy to a very small room or partitioned-off area and cover the floor with newspaper. Make this area large enough so that the puppy will not have to relieve himself next to his bed or his food or water bowls. You will soon find that the puppy will be inclined to use one particular spot to perform his bowel and bladder functions. When you are home you must take the puppy to this exact spot to eliminate at the appropriate time.

Don't let life pass your Eskie by! Proper training will allow him to participate in all the excitement life has to offer.

BASIC TRAINING

The environment in which you train is just as important to your dog's training as your dog's state of mind at the time. Never begin training when you are irritated, distressed, or preoccupied. Nor should you begin basic training in a place that interferes with you or your dog's concentration. Once the commands are understood and learned you can begin testing your dog in public places, but at first the two of you should work in a place where you can concentrate on each other and the lesson at hand.

You must stay aware of an Eskie's sensitivity level and his desire to please. Never resort to striking your Eskie puppy. A very stern "No!" is usually more than sufficient.

The No! Command

There is no doubt whatsoever that one of the most important commands your puppy will ever learn is the

meaning of the no! command. It is critical that the puppy
learns this command just as soon as possible. One important
piece of advice in using this and all other commands—*never
give a command you are not prepared and able to enforce!* A
good leader does not enforce rules arbitrarily. The only way a
puppy learns to obey commands is to realize that once
issued, commands must be complied with. Learning the no
command should start on the first day of the puppy's arrival
at your home.

Leash Training

Begin leash training by putting a soft, light collar on your
puppy. After a few hours of occasional scratching at the
unaccustomed addition, your puppy will quickly forget it is
even there.

It may not be necessary for the puppy or adult Eskie to wear
his collar and identification tags within the confines of your
home. But no dog should ever leave home without a collar and
without an attached leash held securely in your hand.

Begin getting your puppy accustomed to his collar by
leaving it on for a few minutes at a time. Gradually extend the
time you leave the collar on. Once this is accomplished, attach
a lightweight leash to the collar while you are playing with the
puppy. Do not try to guide the puppy at first. You are only
trying to get the puppy used to having something attached to
the collar.

Have your puppy follow you as you move around by
coaxing him along with a treat of some kind. Let the puppy
smell what you have in your hand and then move a few steps
back holding the treat in front of the puppy's nose. As soon as
the puppy takes a few steps toward you, praise him
enthusiastically and continue to do so as you move along.

Make the first few lessons brief and fun for your puppy.
Continue the lessons in your home or yard until he is
completely unconcerned about the fact that he is on a
leash. With a treat in one hand and the leash in the other,
you can begin to use both to guide the puppy in the
direction you wish to go. Eventually the two of you can
venture out on the sidewalk in front of your house and then
on to adventures everywhere! This is one lesson no puppy
is too young to learn.

The Come Command

The next most important lesson for the Eskie puppy to learn is to come when called. Therefore, it is very important that your puppy learn his name as soon as possible. Constant repetition is what does the trick when teaching a puppy his name. Use the name every time you talk to your puppy.

Learning to come on command could save your Eskie's life when the two of you venture out into the world. Your dog must understand that the come command has to be obeyed without question, but the dog should not associate that command with fear. Your Eskie's response to his name and the word "come" should always be associated with a pleasant experience such as great praise and petting or even a food treat.

Again, remember that it is much easier to avoid the establishment of bad habits than it is to correct them once set. *Never* give the come command unless you are sure your puppy will come to you. The very young puppy is far more inclined to respond to

Bonding is by far one of the most important building blocks of training. Karuk's Snowy River revels in the love and attention he gets from his owner Pat Brabant.

learning the come command than the older dog. Young puppies are entirely dependent on you. An older dog may lose some of that dependency and become preoccupied with his surroundings. So start your come-on-command training early.

Use the command initially when the puppy is already on his way to you or give the command while walking or running away from the youngster. Clap your hands and sound very happy and excited about having the puppy join in on this "game."

Basic obedience training is necessary for your dog, not only to teach him acceptable behavior, but to keep him safe as well.

The very young Eskie puppy will normally want to stay as close to his owner as possible, especially in strange surroundings. When your Eskie puppy sees you moving away, his natural inclination will be to get close to you. This is a perfect time to use the come command.

You may want to attach a long leash or rope to the puppy's collar to ensure the correct response. Do not chase or punish your puppy for not obeying the come command. Doing so in the initial stages of training makes the youngster associate the command with something to fear and this will result in avoidance rather than the immediate positive response you desire. It is imperative that you praise your Eskie puppy and give him a treat when he does come to you, even if he voluntarily delays responding for many minutes.

There are basic commands that every dog should know how to perform. This American Eskimo Dog is learning the sit-stay command.

The Sit and Stay Commands

The sit and stay commands are just as important to your Eskie's safety as the no! command and learning to come when called. Even very young Eskies can learn the sit command quickly, especially if it appears to be a game and a food treat is involved.

First, remember that the Eskie-in-training should always be on collar and leash for lessons. An Eskie puppy is curious about everything that goes on around him, and a puppy is not beyond getting up and walking away from his lesson when he has decided he needs to investigate something.

Give the sit command just before you reach down and exert light pressure on your puppy's rear. Praise the puppy profusely when he does sit, even though it was you who exerted the effort. A food treat of some kind always seems to make the experience that more enjoyable for the puppy.

Continue holding the dog's rear end down and repeat the sit command several times. If your puppy makes an attempt to get up, repeat the command yet again while exerting light pressure on the rear end until the correct position is assumed. Make your puppy stay in this position a little bit longer with each succeeding lesson. Begin with a few seconds and increase the time as lessons progress over the following weeks.

Should your puppy attempt to get up or lie down he should be corrected by saying, "Sit!" in a firm voice. This should be accompanied by returning the dog to the desired position. Only when *you* decide that your dog should get up should he be allowed to do so. Do not test your young Eskie puppy's patience. Remember that you are dealing with a baby and that the attention span of any youngster is relatively limited. When you do decide the dog can get up, call his name, say "OK," and make a big fuss over him. Praise and a food treat are in order every time your Eskie responds correctly.

Once your puppy has mastered the sit lesson you may start on the stay command. With your Eskie puppy on leash and facing you, command him to sit, then take a step or two back. If your dog attempts to get up to follow, firmly say, "Sit, stay!" While you are saying this raise your hand, palm toward the dog, and again command "Stay!"

If your dog attempts to get up you must correct him at once, returning him to the sit position and repeating, "Stay!" Once your Eskie begins to understand what you want, you can gradually increase the distance you step back. With a long leash attached to your dog's collar, start with a few steps and gradually increase the distance to several yards. It is important that your dog learn that the sit, stay command must be obeyed no matter how far away you are. With advanced training your Eskie can be taught that the command is to be obeyed even when you leave the room or are entirely out of sight.

There are all kinds of flying disks for dogs, but only one is made with strength, scent, and originality. The Nylabone® Frisbee™* is a must if you want to have this sort of fun with your Eskie. *The trademark Frisbee is under license from Mattel, Inc., California, USA.

As your Eskie becomes accustomed to responding to this lesson and is able to remain in the sit position for as long as you command, do not end the command by calling the dog to you. Walk back to your puppy and say "OK." This will let your dog know the command is over. When your Eskie becomes entirely dependable in this lesson you can then call the dog to you.

The Hercules™ is made of very tough polyurethane. It is designed for Eskies, who are extremely strong chewers. The raised dental tips massage the gums and remove the plaque they encounter during chewing.

The sit, stay command can take considerable time and patience to get across to puppies. You must not forget their attention span will be short. Keep the stay part of the lesson very short until your puppy is about six months old.

The Down Command

Do not try to teach your Eskie puppy too many things at once. Wait until you have mastered one lesson quite well before moving on to something new.

When you feel quite confident that your puppy is comfortable with the sit and stay commands, you can start work on down. This is the single word command for lie down. Use the down command *only* when you want the dog to lie down. If you want your Eskie to get off your sofa or to stop jumping up on people, use the off command. Do not interchange these two commands. Doing so will only serve to confuse your dog and then evoking the right response will become next to impossible.

The down position is especially useful if you want your Eskie to remain in one place for a long period of time. Most dogs are far more inclined to stay put when lying down than when they are sitting or standing.

Teaching this command to your Eskie may take more time and patience than the previous lessons the two of you have undertaken. It is believed by some animal behaviorists that assuming the down position somehow represents submissiveness.

With your Eskie sitting in front of and facing you, hold a treat in your right hand and the excess part of the leash in your left hand. Hold the treat under the dog's nose and slowly bring your hand down to the ground. Your dog will follow the treat with his head and neck. As he does, give the command "down" and exert *light* pressure on the dog's shoulders with your left hand. If your dog resists the pressure on his shoulders, *do not continue pushing down,* doing so will only create more resistance. Reach down and slide the dog's feet toward you until he is lying down.

An alternative method of getting your Eskie headed into the down position is to move around to the dog's right side, and as you draw his attention downward with your right hand, slide your left hand under the dog's front legs and gently slide them forward. You will undoubtedly have to be on your knees next to a Miniature or Toy youngster in order to do this.

As your Eskie's forelegs begin to slide out, keep moving the treat along the ground until the dog's whole body is lying on the ground while you continually repeat "Down." Once your dog has assumed the position you desire, give him the treat and a lot of praise. Continue assisting your puppy into the down position until he does so on his own. Be firm and be patient.

A Circle B Kennels champion sets out to prove that American Eskimo Dogs can do anything— even walk on two feet!

The Heel Command

In learning to heel, your Eskie will walk on your left side with his shoulder next to your leg no matter what direction you might go or how quickly you turn. Teaching your Eskie to heel is critical to off-leash control and will not only make your daily on-leash walks far more enjoyable, it will make a far more tractable companion when the two of you are in crowded or confusing situations. We do not recommend ever allowing your Eskie to be off leash when your are away from home, but it is important to know you can control your dog no matter what the circumstances are.

Although your puppy will want to learn what you have to teach him, keep in mind that his attention span is short and he will need plenty of repetition and praise.

A lightweight, link-chain training collar is best to use for the heel lesson, and changing to this collar for the lesson indicates what you are doing is "business" and not just a casual stroll. These link-chain collars provide both quick pressure around the neck and a snapping sound, both of which get a dog's attention. These collars are sometimes called "choke collars," but rest assured that when the link-chain collar is used properly, it will not choke the dog. The pet shop where you purchase this training collar will be able to show you the proper way to put it on your dog.

As you train your Eskie puppy to walk on the leash, get him accustomed to walking on your left side. The leash should cross your body from the dog's collar to your right hand. The excess portion of the leash will be folded into your right hand and your left hand on the leash will be used to make corrections with the leash.

A quick short jerk on the leash with your left hand will keep your puppy from lunging side to side, pulling ahead, or lagging back. As you make a correction, give the "heel" command. Keep the leash loose when your dog maintains the proper position at your side.

If your dog begins to drift away, give the leash a sharp jerk, guide the dog back to the correct position, and give the "heel" command. Do not pull on the lead with steady pressure. What is needed is a sharp but gentle jerking motion to get your dog's attention.

Training Classes

There are few limits to what a patient, consistent American Eskimo owner can teach his or her dog. Eskies are highly trainable. Remember the breed's heritage. Once lessons are mastered you will find that most Eskies will perform with enough enthusiasm and gusto to make all the hard work worthwhile.

For advanced obedience work beyond the basics, it is wise for the Eskie owner to consider local professional assistance. Professional trainers have had long-standing experience in avoiding the pitfalls of obedience training and can help you to avoid them as well.

This training assistance can be obtained in many ways. Classes are particularly good in that your dog is learning to obey commands in spite of all the interesting sights and smells of other dogs. There are free-of-charge classes at many parks and recreation facilities, as well as very formal and sometimes very expensive individual lessons with private trainers.

There are also some obedience schools that will take your Eskie and train him for you. However, unless your schedule provides no time at all to train your dog, having someone else train the dog for you would be last on our list of recommendations. The rapport that develops between the owner who has trained his or her Eskie and the dog himself is incomparable. The effort you expend to teach your dog to be a pleasant companion and good canine citizen pays off in years of enjoyable companionship.

Versatility

There is no end to the number of activities you and your

American Eskimo can enjoy together. The breed is highly successful in both conformation shows and obedience trials.

There are Canine Good Citizen certificates that can be earned at conformation shows. An event called agility, which is actually an "obstacle course" for dogs, is not only fun for dogs and owners, but Eskie owners find their dogs particularly well suited for this event.

Owners not inclined toward competitive events might find enjoyment in having their Eskie's serve as therapy dogs. Dogs used in this area are trained to assist the sick, the elderly, and often the handicapped. Other therapy dogs make visits to hospitals and homes for the aged. It has been proven these visits provide great therapeutic value to patients.

The time you invest in training your American Eskimo Dog will benefit the both of you for a lifetime. This Eskie easily soars over the bar jump in an agility trial.

The well-trained American Eskimo can provide a whole world of activities for the owner. You are limited only by the amount of time you wish to invest in this remarkable breed.

SPORT of Purebred Dogs

Welcome to the exciting and sometimes frustrating sport of dogs. No doubt you are trying to learn more about dogs or you wouldn't be deep into this book. This section covers the basics that may entice you, further your knowledge and help you to understand the dog world.

Dog showing has been a very popular sport for a long time and has been taken quite seriously by some. Others only enjoy it as a hobby.

The Kennel Club in England was formed in 1859, the American Kennel Club was established in 1884 and the Canadian Kennel Club was formed in 1888. The purpose of these clubs was to register purebred dogs and maintain their Stud Books. In the beginning, the concept of registering dogs was not readily accepted. More than 36 million dogs have been enrolled in the AKC Stud Book since its inception in 1888. Presently the kennel clubs not only register dogs but adopt and enforce rules and regulations governing dog shows, obedience trials and field trials. Over the years they have fostered and encouraged interest in the health and welfare of the purebred dog. They routinely donate funds to veterinary research for study on genetic disorders.

Below are the addresses of the kennel clubs in the United States, Great Britain and Canada.

The American Kennel Club
51 Madison Avenue
New York, NY 10010
(Their registry is located at: 5580 Centerview Drive, STE 200, Raleigh, NC 27606-3390)

The Kennel Club
1 Clarges Street
Piccadilly, London, WIY 8AB, England

The Canadian Kennel Club
111 Eglinton Avenue
East Toronto, Ontario M6S 4V7
Canada

Today there are numerous activities that are enjoyable for both the dog and the handler. Some of the activities include conformation showing, obedience competition, tracking, agility, the Canine Good Citizen Certificate, and a wide range of instinct tests that vary from breed to breed. Where you start depends upon your goals which early on may not be readily apparent.

This American Eskimo puppy is ready for puppy kindergarten—he even has his school bag packed!

PUPPY KINDERGARTEN

Every puppy will benefit from this class. PKT is the foundation for all future dog activities from

conformation to "couch potatoes." Pet owners should make an effort to attend even if they never expect to show their dog. The class is designed for puppies about three months of age with graduation at approximately five months of age. All the puppies will be in the same age group and, even though some may be a little unruly, there should not be any real problem. This class will teach the puppy some beginning obedience. As in all obedience classes the owner learns how to train his own dog. The PKT class gives the puppy the opportunity to interact with other puppies in the same age group and exposes him to strangers, which is very important. Some dogs grow up with behavior problems, one of them being fear of strangers. As you can see, there can be much to gain from this class.

There are some basic obedience exercises that every dog should learn. Some of these can be started with puppy kindergarten.

If you are patient and consistent when training your puppy, you'll have a well-behaved adult Eskie as a reward.

Sit

One way of teaching the sit is to have your dog on your left side with the leash in your right hand, close to the collar. Pull up on the leash and at the same time reach around his hindlegs with your left hand and tuck them in. As you are doing this say, "Beau, sit." Always use the dog's name when you give an active command. Some owners like to use a treat holding it over the dog's head. The dog will need to sit to get the treat. Encourage the dog to hold the sit for a few seconds, which will eventually be the beginning of the Sit/Stay. Depending on how cooperative he is, you can rub him under the chin or stroke his back. It is a good time to establish eye contact.

Down

Sit the dog on your left side and kneel down beside him with the leash in your right hand. Reach over him with your left hand and grasp his left foreleg. With your right hand, take his right foreleg and pull his legs forward while you say, "Beau, down." If he tries to get up, lean on his shoulder to encourage him to stay down. It will relax your dog if you stroke his back while he is down. Try to encourage him to stay down for a few seconds as preparation for the Down/Stay.

Heel

The definition of heeling is the dog walking under control at your left heel. Your puppy will learn controlled walking in the puppy kindergarten class, which will eventually lead to heeling. The command is "Beau, heel," and you start off briskly with your left foot. Your leash is in your right hand and your left hand is holding it about half way down. Your left hand should be able to control the leash and there should be a little slack in it. You want him to walk with you with your leg somewhere between his nose and his shoulder. You need to encourage him to stay with you, not forging (in front of you) or lagging behind you. It is best to keep him on a fairly short lead. Do not allow the lead to become tight. It is far better to give him a little jerk when necessary and remind him to heel. When you come to a halt, be prepared physically to make him sit. It takes practice to become coordinated. There are excellent books on training that you may wish to purchase. Your instructor should be able to recommend one for you.

Recall

This quite possibly is the most important exercise you will ever teach. It should be a pleasant

Group training sessions are a wonderful way for your Eskie to make friends and continue socialization.

Look at those sad Eskie eyes! Be sure to offer your Eskie plenty of positive reinforcement, and in no time at all he'll be obeying every command.

experience. The puppy may learn to do random recalls while being attached to a long line such as a clothes line. Later the exercise will start with the dog sitting and staying until called. The command is "Beau, come." Let your command be happy. You want your dog to come willingly and faithfully. The recall could save his life if he sneaks out the door. In practicing the recall, let him jump on you or touch you before you reach for him. If he is shy, then kneel down to his level. Reaching for the insecure dog could frighten him, and he may not be willing to come again in the future. Lots of praise and a treat would be in order whenever you do a recall. Under no circumstances should you ever correct your dog when he has come to you. Later in formal obedience your dog will be required to sit in front of you after recalling and then go to heel position.

CONFORMATION

Conformation showing is our oldest dog show sport. This type of showing is based on the dog's appearance—that is his structure, movement and attitude. When considering this type of showing, you need to be aware of your breed's standard and be able to evaluate your dog compared to that standard. The breeder of your puppy or other experienced breeders would be good sources for such an evaluation. Puppies can go through lots of changes over a period of time. Many puppies start out as promising hopefuls and then after maturing may be disappointing as show candidates. Even so this should not deter them from being excellent pets.

Usually conformation training classes are offered by the local kennel or obedience clubs. These are excellent places for training puppies. The puppy should be able to walk on a lead before entering such a class. Proper ring procedure and technique for posing (stacking) the dog will be demonstrated as well as gaiting the dog. Usually certain patterns are used in the ring such as the triangle or the "L." Conformation class, like the PKT class, will give your youngster the opportunity to socialize with different breeds of dogs and humans too.

POPpups™ are healthy treats for your American Eskimo Dog. When bone-hard they help to control plaque buildup; when microwaved they become a rich cracker that your Eskie will love. The POPpup™ is available in chicken and other flavors and is fortified with calcium.

In conformation, your American Eskimo Dog is judged by how closely he conforms to the breed standard.

It takes some time to learn the routine of conformation showing. Usually one starts at the puppy matches that may be AKC Sanctioned or Fun Matches. These matches are generally for puppies from two or three months to a year old, and there may be classes for the adult over the age of 12 months. Similar to point shows, the classes are divided by sex and after completion of the classes in that breed or variety, the class winners compete for Best of Breed or Variety. The winner goes on to compete in the Group and the Group winners compete for Best in Match. No championship points are awarded for match wins.

A few matches can be great training for puppies even though there is no intention to go on showing. Matches enable the puppy to meet new people and be handled by a stranger—the judge. It is also a change of environment, which broadens the horizon for both dog and handler. Matches and other dog activities boost the confidence of the handler and especially the younger handlers.

Earning an AKC championship is built on a point system, which is different from Great Britain. To become an AKC Champion of Record the dog must earn 15 points. The number of points earned each time depends upon the number of dogs in competition. The number of points available at each show depends upon the breed, its sex and the location of the show. The United States is divided into ten AKC zones. Each zone has its own set of points. The purpose of the zones is to try to equalize the points available from breed to breed and area to area.The AKC adjusts the point scale annually.

The number of points that can be won at a show are between one and five. Three-, four- and five-point wins are considered majors. Not only does the dog need 15 points won under three different judges, but those points must include two majors under two different judges. Canada also works on a point system but majors are not required.

Dogs always show before bitches. The classes available to those seeking points are: Puppy (which may be divided into 6 to 9 months and 9 to 12 months); 12 to 18 months; Novice; Bred-by-Exhibitor; American-bred; and Open. The class winners of the same sex of each breed or variety compete against each other for Winners Dog and Winners Bitch. A Reserve Winners Dog and Reserve Winners Bitch are also awarded but do not carry any points unless the Winners win is disallowed by AKC. The Winners Dog and Bitch compete with the specials (those dogs that have attained championship) for Best of Breed or Variety, Best of Winners and Best of Opposite Sex. It is possible to pick up an extra point or even a major if the points are higher for the defeated winner than those of Best of Winners. The latter would get the higher total from the defeated winner.

At an all-breed show, each Best of Breed or Variety winner will go on to his respective Group and then the Group winners will compete against each other for Best in Show. There are seven Groups: Sporting, Hounds, Working, Terriers, Toys, Non-Sporting and Herding. Obviously there are no Groups at speciality shows (those shows that have only one breed or a show such as the American Spaniel Club's Flushing Spaniel Show, which is for all flushing spaniel breeds).

Earning a championship in England is somewhat different since they do not have a point system. Challenge Certificates are awarded if the judge feels the dog is deserving regardless of the number of dogs in competition. A dog must earn three Challenge Certificates under three different judges, with at least one of these Certificates being won after the age of 12 months. Competition is very strong and entries may be higher than they are in the U.S. The Kennel Club's Challenge Certificates are only available at Championship Shows.

In England, The Kennel Club regulations require that certain dogs, Border Collies and Gundog breeds, qualify in a working capacity (i.e., obedience or field trials) before becoming a full Champion. If they do not qualify in the working aspect, then they are designated a Show Champion, which is equivalent to the AKC's Champion of Record. A Gundog may be granted the title of Field Trial Champion (FT Ch.) if it passes all the tests in the field but would also have to qualify in conformation before becoming a full Champion. A Border Collie that earns the title of Obedience Champion (Ob Ch.) must

The American Eskimo Dog is shown as part of the Non-Sporting Group at AKC dog shows.

also qualify in the conformation ring before becoming a Champion.

The U.S. doesn't have a designation full Champion but does award for Dual and Triple Champions. The Dual Champion must be a Champion of Record, and either Champion Tracker, Herding Champion, Obedience Trial Champion or Field Champion. Any dog that has been awarded the titles of Champion of Record, and any two of the following: Champion Tracker, Herding Champion, Obedience Trial Champion or Field Champion, may be designated as a Triple Champion.

The shows in England seem to put more emphasis on breeder judges than those in the U.S. There is much competition within the breeds. Therefore the quality of the individual breeds should be very good. In the United States we tend to have more "all around judges" (those that judge multiple breeds) and use the breeder judges at the specialty shows. Breeder judges are more familiar with their own breed since they are actively breeding that breed or did so at one time. Americans emphasize Group and Best in Show wins and promote them accordingly.

The shows in England can be very large and extend over several days, with the Groups being scheduled on different days. Though multi-day shows are not common in the U.S., there are cluster shows, where several different clubs will use the same show site over consecutive days.

Westminster Kennel Club is our most prestigious show although the entry is limited to 2500. In recent years, entry has been limited to Champions. This show is more formal than the majority of the shows with the judges wearing formal attire and the handlers fashionably dressed. In most instances the quality of the dogs is superb. After all, it is a show of Champions. It is a good show to study the AKC registered breeds and is by far the most exciting—especially since it is televised! WKC is one of the few shows in this country that is still benched. This means the dog must be in his benched area during the show hours except when he is being groomed, in the ring, or being exercised.

Typically, the handlers are very particular about their appearances. They are careful not to wear something that will detract from their dog but will

Successful showing requires dedication and preparation, but most of all, it should be an enjoyable experience for handlers and dogs alike.

Handlers must pose their American Eskimo Dogs in the most flattering position to emphasize the dog's specific strengths.

perhaps enhance it. American ring procedure is quite formal compared to that of other countries. There is a certain etiquette expected between the judge and exhibitor and among the other exhibitors. Of course it is not always the case but the judge is supposed to be polite, not engaging in small talk or acknowledging how well he knows the handler. There is a more informal and relaxed atmosphere at the shows in other countries. For instance, the dress code is more casual. I can see where this might be more fun for the exhibitor and especially for the novice. The U.S. is very handler-oriented in many of the breeds. It is true, in most instances, that the experienced professional handler can present the dog better and will have a feel for what a judge likes.

In England, Crufts is The Kennel Club's own show and is most assuredly the largest dog show in the world. They've been known to have an entry of nearly 20,000, and the show lasts four days. Entry is only gained by qualifying through winning in specified classes at another Championship Show. Westminster is strictly conformation, but Crufts exhibitors and spectators enjoy not only conformation but obedience, agility and a multitude of exhibitions as well. Obedience was admitted in 1957 and agility in 1983.

If you are handling your own dog, please give some consideration to your apparel. For sure the dress code at matches is more informal than the point shows. However, you should wear something a little more appropriate than beach attire or ragged jeans and bare feet. If you check out the handlers and see what is presently fashionable, you'll catch on. Men usually dress with a shirt and tie and a nice sports coat. Whether you are male or female, you will want to wear comfortable clothes and shoes. You need to be able to run with your dog and you certainly don't want to take a chance of falling and hurting yourself. Heaven forbid, if nothing else, you'll upset your dog. Women usually wear a dress or two-piece outfit, preferably with pockets to carry bait, comb, brush, etc. In this case men are the lucky ones with all their pockets. Ladies, think about where your dress will be if you need to kneel on the floor and also think about running. Does it allow freedom to do so?

You need to take along dog; crate; ex pen (if you use one); extra newspaper; water pail and water; all required grooming equipment, including hair dryer and extension cord; table; chair for you; bait for dog and lunch for you and friends; and, last but not least, clean up materials, such as plastic bags, paper towels, and perhaps a bath towel and some shampoo—just in case. Don't forget your entry confirmation and directions to the show.

If you are showing in obedience, then you will want to wear pants. Many of our top obedience handlers wear pants that are color-coordinated with their dogs. The philosophy is that imperfections in the black dog will be less obvious next to your black pants.

Whether you are showing in conformation, Junior Showmanship or

Chooz™ are healthy and tasty treats for your American Eskimo Dog because they love cheese. Chooz™ are bone-hard but can be microwaved to expand into a huge, crispy dog biscuit. They are almost fat free and about 70 percent protein.

obedience, you need to watch the clock and be sure you are not late. It is customary to pick up your conformation armband a few minutes before the start of the class. They will not wait for you and if you are on the show grounds and not in the ring, you will upset everyone. It's a little more complicated picking up your obedience armband if you show later in the class. If you have not picked up your armband and they get to your number, you may not be allowed to show. It's best to pick up your armband early, but then you may show earlier than expected if other handlers don't pick up. Customarily all conflicts should be discussed with the judge prior to the start of the class.

Katie Robbins and her eight-week-old friend "Biscuit" share a moment together.

Junior Showmanship

The Junior Showmanship Class is a wonderful way to build self confidence even if there are no aspirations of staying with the dog-show game later in life. Frequently, Junior Showmanship becomes the background of those who become successful exhibitors/handlers in the future. In some instances it is taken very seriously, and success is measured in terms of wins. The Junior Handler is judged solely on his ability and skill in presenting his dog. The dog's conformation is not to be considered by the judge. Even so the condition and grooming of the dog may be a reflection upon the handler.

Usually the matches and point shows include different classes. The Junior Handler's dog may be entered in a breed or obedience class and even shown by another person in that class. Junior Showmanship classes are usually divided by age and perhaps sex. The age is determined by the handler's age on the day of the show. The classes are:

Novice Junior for those at least ten and under 14 years of age who at time of entry closing have not won three first places in a Novice Class at a licensed or member show.

Novice Senior for those at least 14 and under 18 years of age who at the time of entry closing have not won three first places in a Novice Class at a licensed or member show.

Open Junior for those at least ten and under 14 years of age who at the time of entry closing have won at least three first places in a Novice Junior Showmanship Class at a licensed or member show with competition present.

Open Senior for those at least 14 and under 18 years of age who at time of entry closing have won at least three first places in a Novice Junior Showmanship Class at a licensed or member show with competition present.

Junior Handlers must include their AKC Junior Handler number on each show entry. This needs to be obtained from the AKC.

CANINE GOOD CITIZEN

The AKC sponsors a program to encourage dog owners to train their dogs. Local clubs perform the pass/fail tests, and dogs who pass are awarded a Canine Good Citizen Certificate. Proof of vaccination is required at the time of participation. The test includes:

1. Accepting a friendly stranger.

Canine good citizens must be able to get along well with other animals and children. This Eskie looks as if he's passed the test!

2. Sitting politely for petting.
3. Appearance and grooming.
4. Walking on a loose leash.
5. Walking through a crowd.
6. Sit and down on command/staying in place.
7. Come when called.
8. Reaction to another dog.
9. Reactions to distractions.
10. Supervised separation.

If more effort was made by pet owners to accomplish these exercises, fewer dogs would be cast off to the humane shelter.

OBEDIENCE

Obedience is necessary, without a doubt, but it can also become a wonderful hobby or even an obsession. Obedience classes and competition can provide wonderful companionship, not only with your dog but with your classmates or fellow competitors. It is always gratifying to discuss your dog's problems with others who have had similar experiences. The AKC acknowledged Obedience around 1936, and it has changed tremendously even though many

Basic training will help your puppy to understand that he must obey your commands—even when he is playing in the snow!

of the exercises are basically the same. Today, obedience competition is just that—very competitive. Even so, it is possible for every obedience exhibitor to come home a winner (by earning qualifying scores) even though he/she may not earn a placement in the class.

Most of the obedience titles are awarded after earning three qualifying scores (legs) in the appropriate class under three different judges. These classes offer a perfect score of 200, which is extremely rare. Each of the class exercises has its own point value. A leg is earned after receiving a score of at least 170 and at least 50 percent of the points available in each exercise. The titles are:

Companion Dog–CD
This is called the Novice Class and the exercises are:

1. Heel on leash and figure 8	40 points
2. Stand for examination	30 points
3. Heel free	40 points
4. Recall	30 points
5. Long sit–one minute	30 points
6. Long down–three minutes	30 points
Maximum total score	200 points

Companion Dog Excellent–CDX
This is the Open Class and the exercises are:

1. Heel off leash and figure 8	40 points
2. Drop on recall	30 points
3. Retrieve on flat	20 points
4. Retrieve over high jump	30 points
5. Broad jump	20 points
6. Long sit–three minutes (out of sight)	30 points
7. Long down–five minutes (out of sight)	30 points
Maximum total score	200 points

Utility Dog–UD
The Utility Class exercises are:

1. Signal Exercise	40 points
2. Scent discrimination-Article 1	30 points
3. Scent discrimination-Article 2	30 points
4. Directed retrieve	30 points
5. Moving stand and examination	30 points
6. Directed jumping	40 points
Maximum total score	200 points

After achieving the UD title, you may feel inclined to go after the UDX and/or OTCh. The UDX (Utility Dog Excellent) title went into effect in January 1994. It is not easily attained. The title requires qualifying simultaneously ten times in Open B and Utility B but not necessarily at consecutive shows.

The OTCh (Obedience Trial Champion) is awarded after the dog has earned his UD and then goes on to earn 100 championship points, a first place in Utility, a first place in Open and another first place in either class. The placements must be won under three different judges at all-breed obedience trials. The points are determined by the number of dogs competing in the Open B and Utility B classes. The OTCh title precedes the dog's name.

Obedience matches (AKC Sanctioned, Fun, and Show and Go) are usually available. Usually they are sponsored by the local obedience clubs. When preparing an obedience dog for a title, you will find matches very helpful. Fun Matches and Show and Go Matches are more lenient in allowing you to make corrections in the ring. This type of training is usually very necessary for the Open and Utility Classes. AKC Sanctioned Obedience Matches do not allow corrections in the ring since they must abide by the AKC Obedience Regulations. If you are interested in showing in obedience, then you should contact the AKC for a copy of the Obedience Regulations.

Agility is just one of the many activities in which American Eskimo Dogs can demonstrate their athletic and competitive prowess.

AGILITY

Agility was first introduced by John Varley in England at the Crufts Dog Show, February 1978, but Peter Meanwell, competitor and judge, actually developed the idea. It was officially recognized in the early '80s. Agility is extremely popular in England and Canada and growing in popularity in the U.S. The AKC acknowledged agility in August 1994. Dogs must be at least 12 months of age to be entered. It is a fascinating sport that the dog, handler and spectators enjoy to the utmost. Agility is a spectator sport! The dog performs off lead. The handler either runs with his dog or positions himself on the course and directs his dog with verbal and hand signals over a timed course over or through a variety of obstacles including a time out or pause. One of the main drawbacks to agility is finding a place to train. The obstacles take up a lot of space and it is very time consuming to put up and take down courses.

The titles earned at AKC agility trials are Novice Agility Dog (NAD), Open Agility Dog (OAD), Agility Dog Excellent (ADX), and Master Agility Excellent (MAX). In order to acquire an agility title, a dog must earn a qualifying score in its respective class on three separate occasions under two different judges. The MAX will be awarded after earning ten qualifying scores in the Agility Excellent Class.

PERFORMANCE TESTS

During the last decade the American Kennel Club has promoted performance tests—those events that test the different breeds' natural abilities. This type of event encourages a handler to devote even more time to his dog and retain the natural instincts of his breed heritage. It is an important part of the wonderful world of dogs.

Agility competitions are growing in popularity. This American Eskimo Dog easily completes one of the tasks in an agility trial.

General Information

Obedience, tracking and agility allow the purebred dog with an Indefinite Listing Privilege (ILP) number or a limited registration to be exhibited and earn titles. Application must be made to the AKC for an ILP number.

The American Kennel Club publishes a monthly *Events* magazine that is part of the *Gazette*, their official journal for the sport of purebred dogs. The *Events* section lists upcoming shows and the secretary or superintendent for them. The majority of the conformation shows in the U.S. are overseen by licensed superintendents. Generally the entry closing date is approximately two-and-a-half weeks before the actual show. Point shows are fairly expensive, while the match shows cost about one third of the point show entry fee. Match shows usually take entries the day of the show but some are pre-entry. The best way to find match show information is through your local kennel club. Upon asking, the AKC can provide you with a list of superintendents, and you can write and ask to be put on their mailing lists.

There are so many activities that your dog can participate in, and the versatile American Eskimo Dog has the ability to excel at them all. Ch. Ann Dee's Mandolin, owned by Ann De Tavernier, practices his flyball technique.

Obedience trial and tracking test information is available through the AKC. Frequently these events are not superintended, but put on by the host club. Therefore you would make the entry with the event's secretary.

As you have read, there are numerous activities you can share with your dog. Regardless what you do, it does take teamwork. Your dog can only benefit from your attention and training. We hope this chapter has enlightened you and hope, if nothing else, you will attend a show here and there. Perhaps you will start with a puppy kindergarten class, and who knows where it may lead!

HEALTH CARE

Veterinary medicine has become far more sophisticated than what was available to our ancestors. This can be attributed to the increase in household pets and consequently the demand for better care for them. Also human medicine has become far more complex. Today diagnostic testing in veterinary medicine parallels human diagnostics. Because of better technology we can expect our pets to live healthier lives thereby increasing their life spans.

THE FIRST CHECK UP

You will want to take your new puppy/dog in for its first check up within 48 to 72 hours after acquiring it. Many breeders strongly recommend this check up and so do the humane shelters. A puppy/dog can appear healthy but

All American Eskimo puppies are cute, but not all are of breeding quality. Reputable breeders will often sell pet-quality pups on the condition that they are spayed or neutered.

it may have a serious problem that is not apparent to the layman. Most pets have some type of a minor flaw that may never cause a real problem.

Unfortunately if he/she should have a serious problem, you

will want to consider the consequences of keeping the pet and the attachments that will be formed, which may be broken prematurely. Keep in mind there are many healthy dogs looking for good homes.

American Eskimo Dogs are active and playful. Any change in behavior should be brought to your veterinarian's attention.

This first check up is a good time to establish yourself with the veterinarian and learn the office policy regarding their hours and how they handle emergencies. Usually the breeder or another conscientious pet owner is a good reference for locating a capable veterinarian. You should be aware that not all veterinarians give the same quality of service. Please do not make your selection on the least expensive clinic, as they may be short changing your pet. There is the possibility that eventually it will cost you more due to improper diagnosis, treatment, etc. If you are selecting a new veterinarian, feel free to ask for a tour of the clinic. You should inquire about making an appointment for a tour since all clinics are working clinics, and therefore may not be available all day for sightseers. You may worry less if you see where your pet will be spending the day if he ever needs to be hospitalized.

THE PHYSICAL EXAM

Your veterinarian will check your pet's overall condition, which includes listening to the heart; checking the respiration; feeling the abdomen, muscles and joints; checking the mouth, which includes the gum color and signs of gum disease along with plaque buildup; checking the ears for signs of an infection or ear mites; examining the eyes; and, last but not least, checking the condition of the skin and coat.

He should ask you questions regarding your pet's eating and elimination habits and invite you to relay your questions. It is a good idea to prepare a list so as not to forget anything. He should discuss the proper diet and the quantity to be fed. If this should differ from your breeder's recommendation, then

Regular medical care is extremely important to the young puppy. Vaccinations and physical exams are part of your Eskie's lifelong maintenance.

you should convey to him the breeder's choice and see if he approves. If he recommends changing the diet, then this should be done over a few days so as not to cause a gastrointestinal upset. It is customary to take in a fresh stool sample (just a small amount) for a test for intestinal parasites. It must be fresh, preferably within 12 hours, since the eggs hatch quickly and after hatching will not be observed under the microscope. If your pet isn't obliging then, usually the technician can take one in the clinic.

Breeding dogs of only the best quality ensures that good health and temperament are passed down to each new generation.

For the sake of your dog as well as the health of your family, you should bring your new Eskie to the veterinarian within three days of his arrival at your home.

IMMUNIZATIONS

It is important that you take your puppy/dog's vaccination record with you on your first visit. In case of a puppy, presumably the breeder has seen to the vaccinations up to the time you acquired custody. Veterinarians differ in their vaccination protocol. It is not unusual for your puppy to have received vaccinations for distemper, hepatitis, leptospirosis, parvovirus and parainfluenza every two to three weeks from the age of five or six weeks. Usually this is a combined injection and is typically called the DHLPP. The DHLPP is given through at least 12 to 14 weeks of age, and it is customary to continue with another parvovirus vaccine at 16 to 18 weeks. You may wonder why so many immunizations are necessary. No one knows for sure when the puppy's maternal antibodies are gone, although it is customarily accepted that distemper antibodies are gone by 12 weeks. Usually parvovirus antibodies are gone by 16 to 18 weeks of age. However, it is possible for the maternal antibodies to be gone at a much earlier age or even a later age. Therefore immunizations are started at an early age. The vaccine will not give immunity as long as there are maternal antibodies.

The rabies vaccination is given at three or six months of age depending on your local laws. A vaccine for bordetella (kennel cough) is advisable and can be given anytime from the age of five weeks. The coronavirus is not commonly given unless there is a problem locally. The Lyme vaccine is necessary in endemic areas. Lyme disease has been reported in 47 states.

Distemper

This is virtually an incurable disease. If the dog recovers, he is subject to severe nervous disorders. The virus attacks every tissue in the body and resembles a bad cold with a fever. It can cause a runny nose and eyes and cause gastrointestinal disorders, including a poor appetite, vomiting and diarrhea. The virus is carried by raccoons, foxes, wolves, mink and other dogs. Unvaccinated youngsters and senior citizens are very susceptible. This is still a common disease.

Hepatitis

This is a virus that is most serious in very young dogs. It is spread by contact with an infected animal or its stool or urine.

The virus affects the liver and kidneys and is characterized by high fever, depression and lack of appetite. Recovered animals may be afflicted with chronic illnesses.

Leptospirosis

This is a bacterial disease transmitted by contact with the urine of an infected dog, rat or other wildlife. It produces severe symptoms of fever, depression, jaundice and internal bleeding and was fatal before the vaccine was developed. Recovered dogs can be carriers, and the disease can be transmitted from dogs to humans.

Bordetella attached to canine cilia. Otherwise known as kennel cough, this disease is highly contagious and should be vaccinated against routinely.

Parvovirus

This was first noted in the late 1970s and is still a fatal disease. However, with proper vaccinations, early diagnosis and prompt treatment, it is a manageable disease. It attacks the bone marrow and intestinal tract. The symptoms include depression, loss of appetite, vomiting, diarrhea and collapse. Immediate medical attention is of the essence.

Rabies

This is shed in the saliva and is carried by raccoons, skunks, foxes, other dogs and cats. It attacks nerve tissue, resulting in paralysis and death. Rabies can be transmitted to people and is virtually always fatal. This disease is reappearing in the suburbs.

Bordetella (Kennel Cough)

The symptoms are coughing, sneezing, hacking and retching accompanied by nasal discharge usually lasting from a few days to several weeks. There are several disease-producing organisms responsible for this disease. The present vaccines are helpful but do not protect for all the strains. It usually is not life threatening but in some instances it can progress to a serious bronchopneumonia. The disease is highly contagious. The vaccination should be given routinely for dogs that come in contact with other dogs, such as through boarding, training class or visits to the groomer.

Coronavirus

This is usually self limiting and not life threatening. It was first noted in the late '70s about a year before parvovirus. The virus produces a yellow/brown stool and there may be depression, vomiting and diarrhea.

Lyme Disease

This was first diagnosed in the United States in 1976 in Lyme, CT in people who lived in close proximity to the deer tick. Symptoms may include acute lameness, fever, swelling of joints and loss of appetite. Your veterinarian can advise you if you live in an endemic area.

After your puppy has completed his puppy vaccinations, you will continue to booster the DHLPP once a year. It is customary to booster the rabies one year after the first vaccine and then, depending on where you live, it should be boostered every year or every three years. This depends on your local laws. The Lyme and corona vaccines are boostered annually and it is recommended that the bordetella be boostered every six to eight months.

ANNUAL VISIT

I would like to impress the importance of the annual check up, which would include the booster vaccinations, check for intestinal parasites and test for heartworm. Today in our very busy world it is rush, rush and see "how much you can get for how little." Unbelievably, some non-veterinary businesses have entered

The deer tick is the most common carrier of Lyme disease. Photo courtesy of Virbac Laboratories, Inc., Fort Worth, Texas.

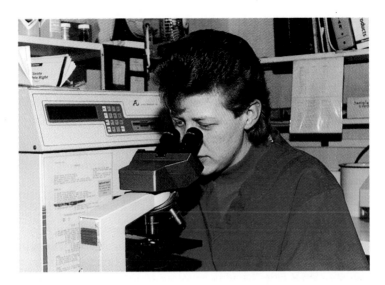

Laboratory tests are studied by highly trained veterinary technicians. Most tests are performed right in your own veterinarian's office.

into the vaccination business. More harm than good can come to your dog through improper vaccinations, possibly from inferior vaccines and/or the wrong schedule. More than likely you truly care about your companion dog and over the years you have devoted much time and expense to his well being. Perhaps you are unaware that a vaccination is not just a vaccination. There is more involved. Please, please follow through with regular physical examinations. It is so important for your veterinarian to know your dog and this is especially true during middle age through the geriatric years. More than likely your older dog will require more than one physical a year. The annual physical is good preventive medicine. Through early diagnosis and subsequent treatment your dog can maintain a longer and better quality of life.

Intestinal Parasites

Hookworms

These are almost microscopic intestinal worms that can cause anemia and therefore serious problems, including death, in young puppies. Hookworms can be transmitted to humans through penetration of the skin. Puppies may be born with them.

Roundworms

These are spaghetti-like worms that can cause a potbellied appearance and dull coat along with more severe symptoms, such as vomiting, diarrhea and coughing. Puppies acquire these while in the mother's uterus and through lactation. Both hookworms and roundworms may be acquired through ingestion.

Whipworms

These have a three-month life cycle and are not acquired through the dam. They cause intermittent diarrhea usually with mucus. Whipworms are possibly the most difficult worm to eradicate. Their eggs are very resistant to most environmental factors and can last for years until the proper conditions enable them to mature. Whipworms are seldom seen in the stool.

Intestinal parasites are more prevalent in some areas than others. Climate, soil and contamination are big factors contributing to the incidence of intestinal parasites. Eggs are passed in the stool, lay on the ground and then become infective in a certain number of days. Each of the above worms has a different life cycle. Your best chance of becoming and remaining worm-free is to always pooper-scoop your yard. A fenced-in yard keeps stray dogs out, which is certainly helpful.

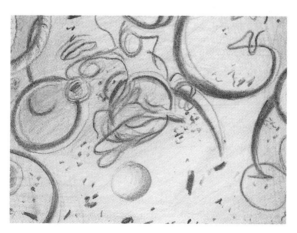

Whipworms are hard to find, and it is a job best left to a veterinarian. Pictured here are adult whipworms.

I would recommend having a fecal examination on your dog twice a year or more often if there is a problem. If your dog has a positive fecal sample, then he will be given the appropriate medication and you will be asked to bring back another stool sample in a certain period of time (depending on the type of worm) and then be rewormed. This process goes on until he has at least two negative samples. The different types of worms require different medications. You will be wasting your money and doing your dog an injustice by buying over-the-counter medication without first consulting your veterinarian.

When visiting the veterinarian, it is customary to take a stool sample to test for intestinal parasites, such as roundworms. Courtesy of Merck AgVet.

Regular visits to the veterinarian will help in the timely diagnosis of any illnesses or parasitic infections.

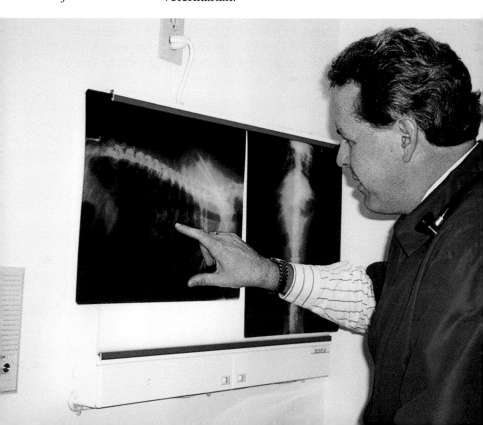

OTHER INTERNAL PARASITES

Coccidiosis and Giardiasis

These protozoal infections usually affect puppies, especially in places where large numbers of puppies are brought together. Older dogs may harbor these infections but do not show signs unless they are stressed. Symptoms include diarrhea, weight loss and lack of appetite. These infections are not always apparent in the fecal examination.

Tapeworms

Seldom apparent on fecal floatation, they are diagnosed frequently as rice-like segments around the dog's anus and the base of the tail. Tapeworms are long, flat and ribbon like, sometimes several feet in length, and made up of many segments about five-eighths of an inch long. The two most common types of tapeworms found in the dog are:

(1) First the larval form of the flea tapeworm parasite must mature in an intermediate host, the flea, before it can become infective. Your dog acquires this by ingesting the flea through licking and chewing.

(2) Rabbits, rodents and certain large game animals serve as intermediate hosts for other species of tapeworms. If your dog should eat one of these infected hosts, then he can acquire tapeworms.

The cat flea is the most common flea of both dogs and cats. Courtesy of Fleabusters, RX for Fleas Inc., Fort Lauderdale, Florida.

HEARTWORM DISEASE

This is a worm that resides in the heart and adjacent blood vessels of the lung that produces microfilaria, which circulate in the bloodstream. It is possible for a dog to be infected with any number of worms from one to a hundred that can be 6 to 14 inches long. It is a life-threatening disease, expensive to treat and easily prevented. Depending on where you live, your veterinarian may recommend a preventive year-round and either an annual or semiannual blood

Dirofilaria—adult worms in the heart of a dog. Courtesy of Merck AgVet.

test. The most common preventive is given once a month.

EXTERNAL PARASITES

Fleas

These pests are not only the dog's worst enemy but also enemy to the owner's pocketbook. Preventing is less expensive than treating, but regardless we'd prefer to spend our money elsewhere. Likely, the majority of our dogs are allergic to the bite of a flea, and in many cases it only takes one flea bite. The protein in the flea's saliva is the culprit. Allergic dogs have a reaction, which usually results in a "hot spot." More than likely such a reaction will involve a trip to the veterinarian for treatment. Yes, prevention is less expensive. Fortunately today there are several good products available.

If there is a flea infestation, no one product is going to correct the problem. Not only will the dog require treatment so will the environment. In general flea collars are not very effective although there is now available an "egg" collar that will kill the eggs on the dog. Dips are the most economical but they are messy. There are some effective shampoos and treatments available through pet shops and veterinarians. An oral tablet arrived on the American market in 1995 and was popular in Europe the previous year. It sterilizes the female flea but will not kill adult fleas. Therefore the tablet, which is given monthly, will decrease the flea population but is not a "cure-all." Those dogs that suffer from flea-bite allergy will still be subjected to the bite of the flea. Another popular parasiticide is permethrin, which is applied to the back of the dog in one or two places depending on the dog's weight. This product works as a repellent causing the flea to get "hot feet" and jump off. Do not confuse this product with some of the organophosphates that are also applied to the dog's back.

Some products are not usable on young puppies. Treating fleas should be done under your veterinarian's guidance. Frequently it is necessary to combine products and the layman does not have the knowledge regarding possible toxicities. It is hard to believe but there are a few dogs that do have a natural resistance to fleas. Nevertheless it would be wise to treat all pets at the same time. Don't forget your cats. Cats just love to prowl the neighborhood and consequently return with unwanted guests.

Adult fleas live on the dog but their eggs drop off the dog into the environment. There they go through four larval stages before reaching adulthood, and thereby are able to jump back on the poor unsuspecting dog. The cycle resumes and takes between 21 to 28 days under ideal conditions. There are environmental products available that will kill both the adult fleas and the larvae.

Ticks

Ticks carry Rocky Mountain Spotted Fever, Lyme disease and can cause tick paralysis. They should be removed with tweezers, trying to pull out the head. The jaws carry disease. There is a tick preventive collar that does an excellent job. The ticks automatically back out on those dogs wearing collars.

Sarcoptic Mange

This is a mite that is difficult to find on skin scrapings. The pinnal reflex is a good indicator of this disease. Rub the ends of the pinna (ear) together and the dog will start scratching with his foot. Sarcoptes are highly contagious to other dogs and to humans although they do not live long on humans. They cause intense itching.

Demodectic Mange

This is a mite that is passed from the dam to her puppies. It affects youngsters age three to ten months. Diagnosis is confirmed by skin scraping. Small areas of alopecia around the eyes, lips and/or forelegs become visible. There is little itching unless there is a secondary bacterial infection. Some breeds are afflicted more than others.

Cheyletiella
This causes intense itching and is diagnosed by skin scraping. It lives in the outer layers of the skin of dogs, cats, rabbits and humans. Yellow-gray scales may be found on the back and the rump, top of the head and the nose.

TO BREED OR NOT TO BREED
More than likely your breeder has requested that you have your puppy neutered or spayed. Your breeder's request is based on what is healthiest for your dog and what is most beneficial for your breed. Experienced and conscientious breeders devote many years into developing a bloodline. In order to do this, he makes every effort to plan each breeding in regard to conformation, temperament and health. This type of breeder does his best to perform the necessary testing (i.e., OFA, CERF, testing for inherited blood disorders, thyroid, etc.). Testing is

Breeding should be attempted only by someone who is conscientious, knowledgeable, and willing to take responsibility for the dogs and new puppies involved.

expensive and sometimes very disheartening when a favorite dog doesn't pass his health tests. The health history pertains not only to the breeding stock but to the immediate ancestors. Reputable breeders do not want their offspring to be bred indiscriminately. Therefore you may be asked to neuter or spay your puppy. Of course there is always the exception, and your breeder may agree to let you breed your dog under his direct supervision. This is an important concept. More and more effort is being made to breed healthier dogs.

Spay/Neuter

There are numerous benefits of performing this surgery at six months of age. Unspayed females are subject to mammary and ovarian cancer. In order to prevent mammary cancer she must be spayed prior to her first heat cycle. Later in life, an unspayed female may develop a pyometra (an infected uterus), which is definitely life threatening.

Spaying is performed under a general anesthetic and is easy on the young dog. As you might expect it is a little harder on the older dog, but that is no reason to deny her the surgery. The surgery removes the ovaries and uterus. It is important to remove all the ovarian tissue. If some is left behind, she could remain attractive to males. In order to view the ovaries, a reasonably long incision is necessary. An ovariohysterectomy is considered major surgery.

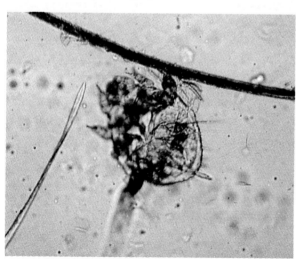

Sarcoptic mange is highly contagious to other dogs as well as humans. Sarcoptes cause intense itching.

Neutering the male at a young age will inhibit some characteristic male behavior that owners frown upon. Some boys will not hike their legs and mark territory if they are neutered at six months of age. Also neutering at a young age has hormonal benefits, lessening the chance of hormonal aggressiveness. Surgery involves removing the testicles but leaving the scrotum. If there should be a retained testicle, then he definitely needs to be neutered before the age of two or three years. Retained testicles can develop into cancer. Unneutered males are at risk for testicular cancer, perineal fistulas, perianal tumors and fistulas and prostatic disease.

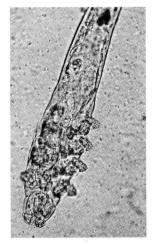

Demodectic mange is passed from a dam to her puppies. It involves areas of hair loss.

Intact males and females are prone to housebreaking accidents. Females urinate frequently before, during and after heat cycles, and males tend to mark territory if there is a female in heat. Males may show the same behavior if there is a visiting dog or guests.

Surgery involves a sterile operating procedure equivalent to human surgery. The incision site is shaved, surgically scrubbed and draped. The veterinarian wears a sterile surgical gown, cap, mask and gloves. Anesthesia should be monitored by a registered technician. It is customary for the veterinarian to recommend a pre-anesthetic blood screening, looking for metabolic problems and a ECG rhythm strip to check for normal heart function. Today anesthetics are equal to human anesthetics, which enables your dog to walk out of the clinic the same day as surgery.

Some folks worry about their dog gaining weight after being neutered or spayed. This is usually not the case. It is true that some dogs may be less active so they could develop a problem, but most dogs are just as active as they were before surgery. However, if your dog should begin to gain, then you need to decrease his food and see to it that he gets a little more exercise.

DENTAL CARE for Your Dog's Life

S o you've got a new puppy! You also have a new set of puppy teeth in your household. Anyone who has ever raised a puppy is abundantly aware of these new teeth. Your puppy will chew anything it can reach, chase your shoelaces, and play "tear the rag" with any piece of clothing it can find. When puppies are newly born, they have no teeth. At about four weeks of age, puppies of most breeds begin to develop their deciduous or baby teeth. They begin eating semi-solid food, fighting and biting with their litter mates, and learning discipline from their mother. As their new teeth come in, they inflict more pain on their mother's breasts, so her feeding sessions become less frequent and shorter. By six or eight weeks, the mother will start growling to warn her pups when they are fighting too roughly or hurting her as they nurse too much with their new teeth.

Puppies need to chew. It is a necessary part of their physical and mental development. They develop muscles and necessary life skills as they drag objects around, fight over possession, and vocalize alerts and warnings. Puppies chew on things to explore their world. They are using their sense of taste to determine what is food and what is not. How else can they tell an electrical cord from a lizard? At about four months of age, most puppies begin shedding their baby teeth. Often these teeth need some help to come out and make way for the permanent teeth. The incisors (front teeth) will be replaced first. Then, the adult canine or fang teeth erupt. When the baby tooth is not shed before the permanent tooth comes in, veterinarians call it a retained deciduous tooth. This condition will often cause gum infections by trapping hair and debris between the permanent tooth and the retained baby tooth. Nylafloss® is an excellent device for puppies to use. They can toss it, drag it, and chew on the many surfaces it presents. The baby teeth can catch in the nylon material, aiding in their removal. Puppies that have adequate chew toys will have less destructive behavior, develop more physically, and have less chance of retained deciduous teeth.

During the first year, your dog should be seen by your veterinarian at regular intervals. Your veterinarian will let you know when to bring in your puppy for vaccinations and parasite examinations. At each visit, your veterinarian should inspect the lips, teeth, and mouth as part of a complete physical examination. You should take some part in the maintenance of your dog's oral health. You should examine your dog's mouth weekly throughout his first year to make sure there are no sores, foreign objects, tooth problems, etc. If your dog drools excessively, shakes its head, or has bad breath, consult your veterinarian. By the time your dog is six months old, the permanent teeth are all in and plaque can start to accumulate on the tooth surfaces. This is when your dog needs to develop good dental-care habits to prevent calculus build-up on its teeth. Brushing is best. That is a fact that cannot be denied. However, some dogs do not like their teeth brushed regularly, or you may not be able to accomplish the task. In that case, you should consider a product that will help prevent plaque and calculus build-up.

Raised dental tips on the surface of every Plaque Attacker™ bone help to combat plaque and tartar. Safe for aggressive chewers and ruggedly constructed to last, Plaque Attacker™ dental bones provide hours and hours of tooth-saving enjoyment.

The Plaque Attackers® and Galileo Bone® are other excellent choices for the first three years of a dog's life. Their shapes make them interesting for the dog. As the dog chews on them, the solid polyurethane massages the gums which improves the blood circulation to the periodontal tissues. Projections on the chew devices increase the surface and are in contact with the tooth for more efficient cleaning. The unique shape and consistency prevent your dog from exerting excessive force on his own teeth or from breaking off pieces of the bone. If your dog is an aggressive chewer or weighs more than 55 pounds (25 kg), you should consider giving him a Nylabone®, the most durable chew product on the market.

The Gumabones®, made by the Nylabone Company, is constructed of strong polyurethane, which is softer than nylon.

Less powerful chewers prefer the Gumabones® to the Nylabones®. A super option for your dog is the Hercules Bone®, a uniquely shaped bone named after the great Olympian for its exception strength. Like all Nylabone products, they are

Nylon is the only material suitable for flossing human teeth. So why not get a chew toy that will enable you to interact with your American Eskimo Dog while it promotes dental health? As you play tug-of-war with a Nylafloss™, you'll be slowly pulling the nylon strand through your dog's teeth.

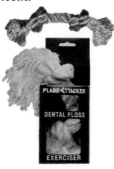

specially scented to make them attractive to your dog. Ask your veterinarian about these bones and he will validate the good doctor's prescription: Nylabones® not only give your dog a good chewing workout but also help to save your dog's teeth (and even his life, as it protects him from possible fatal periodontal diseases).

By the time dogs are four years old, 75% of them have periodontal disease. It is the most common infection in dogs. Yearly examinations by your veterinarian are essential to maintaining your dog's good health. If your veterinarian detects periodontal disease, he or she may recommend a prophylactic cleaning. To do a thorough cleaning, it will be necessary to put your dog under anesthesia. With modern gas anesthetics and monitoring equipment, the procedure is pretty safe. Your veterinarian will scale the teeth with an ultrasound scaler or hand instrument. This removes the calculus from the teeth. If there are calculus deposits below the gum line, the veterinarian will plane the roots to make them smooth. After all of the calculus has been removed, the teeth are polished with pumice in a polishing cup. If any medical or surgical treatment is needed, it is done at this time. The final step would be fluoride treatment and your follow-up treatment at home. If the periodontal disease is advanced, the veterinarian may prescribe a medicated mouth rinse or antibiotics for use at home. Make sure your dog has safe, clean and attractive chew toys and treats. Chooz® treats are another way of using a consumable treat to help keep your dog's teeth clean.

Rawhide is the most popular of all materials for a dog to chew. This has never been good news to dog owners, because rawhide is inherently very dangerous for dogs. Thousands of dogs have died from rawhide, having swallowed the hide after it has become soft and mushy, only to cause stomach and intestinal blockage. A new rawhide product on the market has finally solved the problem of rawhide: molded Roar-Hide® from Nylabone. These are composed of processed, cut up, and melted American rawhide injected into your dog's favorite shape: a dog bone. These dog-safe devices smell and taste like rawhide but don't break up. The ridges on the bones help to fight tartar build-up on the teeth and they last ten times longer than the usual rawhide chews.

Brushing your dog's teeth is recommended by many veterinarians. Use the 2-Brush™ regularly, and you may never need your veterinarian to do the job for you.

As your dog ages, professional examination and cleaning should become more frequent. The mouth should be inspected at least once a year. Your veterinarian may recommend visits every six months. In the geriatric patient, organs such as the heart, liver, and kidneys do not function as well as when they were young. Your veterinarian will probably want to test these organs' functions prior to using general anesthesia for dental cleaning. If your dog is a good chewer and you work closely with your veterinarian, your dog can keep all of its teeth all of its life. However, as your dog ages, his sense of smell, sight, and taste will diminish. He may not have the desire to chase, trap or chew his toys. He will also not have the energy to chew for long periods, as arthritis and periodontal disease make chewing painful. This will leave you with more responsibility for keeping his teeth clean and healthy. The dog that would not let you brush his teeth at one year of age, may let you brush his teeth now that he is ten years old.

If you train your dog with good chewing habits as a puppy, he will have healthier teeth throughout his life.

TRAVELING with Your Dog

The earlier you start traveling with your new puppy or dog, the better. He needs to become accustomed to traveling. However, some dogs are nervous riders and become carsick easily. It is helpful if he starts with an empty stomach. Do not despair, as it will go better if you continue taking him with you on short fun rides. How would you feel if every time you rode in the car you stopped at the doctor's for an injection? You would soon dread that nasty car. Older dogs that tend to get carsick may have more of a problem adjusting to traveling. Those dogs that are having a serious problem may benefit from some medication prescribed by the veterinarian.

Before any car excursion, be sure to allow your Eskies plenty of time outdoors to attend to their needs.

The earlier you take your American Eskimo Dogs traveling with you, the quicker they will become accustomed to riding in a car.

Do give your dog a chance to relieve himself before getting into the car. It is a good idea to be prepared for a clean up with a leash, paper towels, bag and terry cloth towel.

The safest place for your dog is in a fiberglass crate, although close confinement can promote carsickness in some dogs. If your dog is nervous you can try letting him ride on the seat next to you or in someone's lap.

An alternative to the crate would be to use a car harness made for dogs and/or a safety strap attached to the harness or collar. Whatever you do, do not let your dog ride in the back of a pickup truck unless he is securely tied on a very short lead. I've seen trucks stop quickly and, even though the dog was tied, it fell out and was dragged.

Another advantage of the crate is that it is a safe place to leave him if you need to run into the store. Otherwise you wouldn't be able to leave the windows down. Keep in mind that while many dogs are overly protective in their crates, this may not be enough to deter dognappers. In some states it is against the law to leave a dog in the car unattended.

Never leave a dog loose in the car wearing a collar and leash. More than one dog has killed himself by hanging. Do not let him put his head out an open window. Foreign debris can be blown into his eyes. When leaving your dog unattended in a car, consider the temperature. It can take less than five minutes to reach temperatures over 100 degrees Fahrenheit.

TRIPS

Perhaps you are taking a trip. Give consideration to what is best for your dog—traveling with you or boarding. When traveling by car, van or motor home, you need to think ahead about locking your vehicle. In all probability you have many valuables in the car and do not wish to leave it unlocked. Perhaps most valuable and not replaceable is your dog. Give thought to securing your vehicle and providing adequate ventilation for him. Another consideration for you when traveling with your dog is medical problems that may arise and little inconveniences, such as exposure to external parasites. Some areas of the country are quite flea infested. You may want to carry flea spray with you. This is even a good idea when staying in motels. Quite possibly you are not the only occupant of the room.

Unbelievably many motels and even hotels do allow canine guests, even some very first-class ones. Gaines Pet Foods Corporation publishes *Touring With Towser*, a directory of domestic hotels and motels that accommodate guests with

dogs. Their address is Gaines TWT, PO Box 5700, Kankakee, IL, 60902. Call ahead to any motel that you may be considering and see if they accept pets. Sometimes it

If you decide to bring your American Eskimo Dog with you when you travel, bring along some familiar things, like his toys, to make him feel more at home.

Crates are a safe way for your dog to travel. The fiberglass crates are the safest for air travel, but the metal crates allow for better air circulation.

is necessary to pay a deposit against room damage. The management may feel reassured if you mention that your dog will be crated. If you do travel with your dog, take along plenty of baggies so that you can clean up after him. When we all do our share in cleaning up, we make it possible for motels to continue accepting our pets. As a matter of fact, you should practice cleaning up everywhere you take your dog.

Depending on where your are traveling, you may need an up-to-date health certificate issued by your veterinarian. It is good policy to take along your dog's medical information, which would include the name, address and phone number of your veterinarian, vaccination record, rabies certificate, and any medication he is taking.

AIR TRAVEL

When traveling by air, you need to contact the airlines to check their policy. Usually you have to make arrangements up to a couple of weeks in advance for traveling with your dog. The airlines require your dog to travel in an airline approved fiberglass crate. Usually these can be purchased through the airlines but they are also readily available in most pet-supply stores. If your dog is not accustomed to a crate, then it is a good idea to get him acclimated to it before your trip. The day of the actual trip you should withhold water about one hour ahead of departure and no food for about 12 hours. The airlines generally have temperature restrictions, which do not allow pets to travel if it is either too cold or too hot. Frequently these restrictions are based on the temperatures at the departure and arrival airports. It's best to inquire about a health certificate. These usually need to be issued within ten days of departure. You should arrange for non-stop, direct flights and if a commuter plane should be involved, check to see if it will carry dogs. Some don't. The Humane Society of the United States has put together a tip sheet for airline traveling. You can receive a copy by sending a self-addressed stamped envelope to:

The Humane Society of the United States
Tip Sheet
2100 L Street NW
Washington, DC 20037.

Regulations differ for traveling outside of the country and are sometimes changed without notice. Well in advance you need to write or call the appropriate consulate or agricultural department for instructions. Some countries have lengthy quarantines (six months), and countries differ in their rabies vaccination requirements. For instance, it may have to be given at least 30 days ahead of your departure.

Do make sure your dog is wearing proper identification including your name, phone number and city. You never know when you might be in an accident and separated from your dog. Or your dog could be frightened and somehow manage to escape and run away.

If your Eskie is more comfortable at home when you travel, there may be a reputable pet-sitting service available in your area.

Another suggestion would be to carry in-case-of-emergency instructions. These would include the address and phone number of a relative or friend, your veterinarian's name, address and phone number, and your dog's medical information.

A reputable boarding kennel will require that dogs receive the vaccination for kennel cough no less than two weeks before their scheduled stay.

BOARDING KENNELS

Perhaps you have decided that you need to board your dog. Your veterinarian can recommend a good boarding facility or possibly a pet sitter that will come to your house. It is customary for the boarding kennel to ask for proof of vaccination for the DHLPP, rabies and bordetella vaccine. The bordetella should have been given within six months of boarding. This is for your protection. If they do not ask for this proof I would not board at their kennel. Ask about flea control. Those dogs that suffer flea-bite allergy can get in trouble at a boarding kennel. Unfortunately boarding kennels are limited on how much they are able to do.

For more information on pet sitting, contact NAPPS:
National Association of Professional Pet Sitters
1200 G Street, NW
Suite 760
Washington, DC 20005.

Some pet clinics have technicians that pet sit and technicians that board clinic patients in their homes. This may be an alternative for you. Ask your veterinarian if they have an employee that can help you. There is a definite advantage of having a technician care for your dog, especially if your dog is on medication or is a senior citizen.

You can write for a copy of *Traveling With Your Pet* from ASPCA, Education Department, 441 E. 92nd Street, New York, NY 10128.

IDENTIFICATION and Finding the Lost Dog

There are several ways of identifying your dog. The old standby is a collar with dog license, rabies, and ID tags. Unfortunately collars have a way of being separated from the dog and tags fall off. We're not suggesting you shouldn't use a collar and tags. If they stay intact and on the dog, they are the quickest way of identification.

For several years owners have been tattooing their dogs. Some tattoos use a number with a registry. Here lies the problem because there are several registries to check. If you wish to tattoo, use your social security number. The humane shelters have the means to trace it. It is usually done on the inside of the rear thigh. The area is first shaved and numbed. There is no pain, although a few dogs do not like the buzzing sound. Occasionally tattooing is not legible and needs to be redone.

The newest method of identification is microchipping. The microchip is no bigger than a grain of rice.

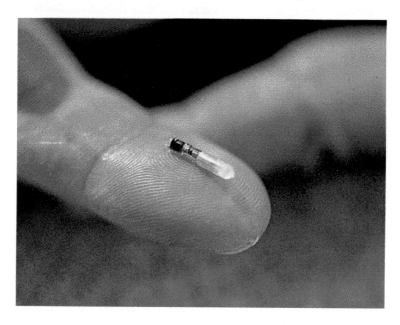

Make sure you have a clear recent picture of your Eskie to distribute in case he becomes lost.

The newest method of identification is microchipping. The microchip is a computer chip that is no larger than a grain of rice. The veterinarian implants it by injection between the shoulder blades. The dog feels no discomfort. If your dog is lost and picked up by the humane society, they can trace you by scanning the microchip, which has its own code. Microchip scanners are friendly to other brands of microchips and their registries. The microchip comes with a dog tag saying the dog is microchipped. It is the safest way of identifying your dog.

FINDING THE LOST DOG

I am sure you will agree that there would be little worse than losing your dog. Responsible pet owners rarely lose their dogs. They do not let their dogs run free because they don't want harm to come to them. Not only that but in most, if not all, states there is a leash law.

Beware of fenced-in yards. They can be a hazard. Dogs find ways to escape either over or under the fence. Another fast exit is through the gate that perhaps the neighbor's child left unlocked.

Below is a list that hopefully will be of help to you if you need it. Remember don't give up, keep looking. Your dog is worth your efforts.

1. Contact your neighbors and put flyers with a photo on it in their mailboxes. Information you should include would be the dog's name, breed, sex, color, age, source of identification, when your dog was last seen and where, and your name and phone numbers. It may be helpful to say the dog needs medical care. Offer a *reward*.

2. Check all local shelters daily. It is also possible for your dog to be picked up away from home and end up in an out-of-the-way shelter. Check these too. Go in person. It is not good enough to call. Most shelters are limited on the time they can hold dogs then they are put up for adoption or euthanized. There is the possibility that your dog will not make it to the shelter for several days. Your dog could

American Eskimo Dogs like to be active. Provide yours with a safe outdoor enclosure for playtime.

have been wandering or someone may have tried to keep him.

3. Notify all local veterinarians. Call and send flyers.

4. Call your breeder. Frequently breeders are contacted when one of their breed is found.

5. Contact the rescue group for your breed.

6. Contact local schools—children may have seen your dog.

7. Post flyers at the schools, groceries, gas stations, convenience stores, veterinary clinics, groomers and any other place that will allow them.

8. Advertise in the newspaper.

9. Advertise on the radio.

Your Eskie will be curious about his environment when you take him out. It is a good idea to keep him on a lead to prevent him from wandering off without you.

When your American Eskimo Dog spends time outdoors, be sure he wears a collar with tags at all times. This will increase your chances of being reunited should you become separated.

BEHAVIOR and Canine Communication

S tudies of the human/animal bond point out the importance of the unique relationships that exist between people and their pets. Those of us who share our lives with pets understand the special part they play through companionship, service and protection. For many, the pet/owner bond goes beyond simple companionship; pets are often considered members of the family. A leading pet food manufacturer recently conducted a nationwide survey of pet owners to gauge just how important pets were in their lives. Here's what they found:

There are many predicaments that your American Eskimo Dog can get into in the great outdoors. Always closely supervise him when outside.

• 76 percent allow their pets to sleep on their beds
• 78 percent think of their pets as their children
• 84 percent display photos of their pets, mostly in their homes
• 84 percent think that their pets react to their own emotions
• 100 percent talk to their pets
• 97 percent think that their pets understand what they're saying
Are you surprised?

Dogs are a very important part of their owners' lives, and the bond between humans and animals is a strong one.

Senior citizens show more concern for their own eating habits when they have the responsibility of feeding a dog. Seeing that their dog is routinely exercised encourages the owner to think of schedules that otherwise may seem unimportant to the senior citizen. The older owner may be arthritic and feeling poorly but with responsibility for his dog he has a reason to get up and get moving. It is a big plus if his dog is an attention seeker who will demand such from his owner.

Over the last couple of decades, it has been shown that pets relieve the stress of those who lead busy lives. Owning a pet has been known to lessen the occurrence of heart attack and stroke.

Many single folks thrive on the companionship of a dog. Lifestyles are very different from a long time ago, and today more individuals seek the single life. However, they receive fulfillment from owning a dog.

Most likely the majority of our dogs live in family environments. The companionship they provide is well worth the effort involved. In my opinion, every child should have the opportunity to have a family dog. Dogs teach responsibility through understanding their care, feelings and even respecting their life cycles. Frequently those children who have not been exposed to dogs grow up afraid of dogs, which isn't good. Dogs sense timidity and some will take advantage of the situation.

Today more dogs are serving as service dogs. Since the origination of the Seeing Eye dogs years ago, we now have trained hearing dogs. Also dogs are trained to provide service for the handicapped and are able to perform many different tasks for their owners. Search and Rescue dogs, with their handlers, are sent throughout the world to assist in recovery of disaster victims. They are life savers.

Therapy dogs are very popular with nursing homes, and some hospitals even allow them to visit. The inhabitants truly look forward to their visits. They wanted and were allowed to have visiting dogs in their beds to hold and love.

Nationally there is a Pet Awareness Week to educate students and others about the value and basic care of our pets. Many countries take an even greater interest in their pets than Americans do. In those countries the pets are allowed to accompany their owners into restaurants and shops, etc. In the U.S. this freedom is only available to our service dogs. Even so we think very highly of the human/animal bond.

Many people thrive on the devoted companionship an American Eskimo Dog can provide. Carolyn Harman and these Kandia Kennels puppies agree!

CANINE BEHAVIOR

Canine behavior problems are the number-one reason for pet owners to dispose of their dogs, either through new homes, humane shelters or euthanasia. Unfortunately there are too many owners who are unwilling to devote the necessary time to properly train their dogs. On the other hand, there are those who not only are concerned about inherited health problems but are also aware of the dog's mental stability.

You may realize that a breed and his group relatives (i.e., sporting, hounds, etc.) show tendencies to behavioral characteristics. An experienced breeder can acquaint you with his breed's personality. Unfortunately many breeds are labeled with poor temperaments when actually the breed as a whole is not affected but only a small percentage of individuals within the breed.

A lot can be learned about an Eskie's behavior and attitude simply by observing his body language. This little guy looks happy and relaxed.

Inheritance and environment contribute to the dog's behavior. Some naïve people suggest inbreeding as the cause of bad temperaments. Inbreeding only results in poor behavior if the ancestors carry the trait. If there are excellent temperaments behind the dogs, then inbreeding will promote good temperaments in the offspring. Did you ever consider that inbreeding is what sets the characteristics of a breed? A purebred dog is the end result of inbreeding. This does not spare the mixed-breed dog from the same problems. Mixed-breed dogs frequently are the offspring of purebred dogs.

Not too many decades ago most of our dogs led a different lifestyle than what is prevalent today. Usually mom stayed home so the dog had human companionship and someone to discipline it if needed. Not much was expected from the dog. Today's mom works and everyone's life is at a much faster pace.

A properly socialized Eskie will be able to get along with all the members of a household. This Eskie and his stuffed armadillo friend enjoy each other's company.

The dog may have to adjust to being a "weekend" dog. The family is gone all day during the week, and the dog is left to his own devices for entertainment. Some dogs sleep all day waiting for their family to come home and others become wigwam wreckers if given the opportunity. Crates do ensure the safety of the dog and the house. However, he could become a physically and emotionally cripple if he doesn't get enough exercise and attention. We still appreciate and want the companionship of our dogs although we expect more from them. In many cases we tend to forget dogs are just that—*dogs* not human beings.

SOCIALIZING AND TRAINING

Many prospective puppy buyers lack experience regarding the proper socialization and training needed to develop the type of pet we all desire. In the first 18 months, training does take some work. It is easier to start proper training before there is a problem that needs to be corrected.

The initial work begins with the breeder. The breeder should start socializing the puppy at five to six weeks of age and cannot let up. Human socializing is critical up through 12 weeks of age and likewise important during the following months. The litter should be left together during the first few weeks but it is necessary to separate them by ten weeks of age. Leaving them together after that time will increase competition for litter dominance. If puppies are not socialized with people by 12 weeks of age, they will be timid in later life.

The eight- to ten-week age period is a fearful time for puppies. They need to be handled very gently around children and adults. There should be no harsh discipline during this time. Starting at 14 weeks of age, the puppy begins the juvenile period, which ends when he reaches sexual maturity around six to 14 months of age. During the juvenile period he needs to

Your puppy's relationship with his littermates is an essential one. He will learn to interact with other dogs by playing with his siblings.

be introduced to strangers (adults, children and other dogs) on the home property. At sexual maturity he will begin to bark at strangers and become more protective. Males start to lift their legs to urinate but if you desire you can inhibit this behavior by walking your boy on leash away from trees, shrubs, fences, etc.

Perhaps you are thinking about an older puppy. You need to inquire about the puppy's social experience. If he has lived in a kennel, he may have a hard time adjusting to people and environmental stimuli. Assuming he has had a good social upbringing, there are advantages to an older puppy.

Training includes puppy kindergarten and a minimum of one to two basic training classes. During these classes you will learn how to dominate your youngster. This is especially important if you own a large breed of dog. It is somewhat harder, if not nearly impossible, for some owners to be the Alpha figure when their dog towers over them. You will be taught how to properly restrain your dog. This concept is important. Again it puts you in the Alpha position. All dogs need to be restrained many times during their lives. Believe it or not, some of our worst offenders are the eight-week-old puppies that are brought to our clinic. They need to be gently restrained for a nail trim but the way they carry on you would think we were killing them. In comparison, their vaccination is a "piece of cake." When we ask dogs to do something that is not agreeable to them, then their worst comes out. Life will be easier for your dog if you expose him at a young age to the necessities of life—proper behavior and restraint.

UNDERSTANDING THE DOG'S LANGUAGE

Most authorities agree that the dog is a descendent of the wolf. The dog and wolf have similar traits. For instance both are pack oriented and prefer not to be isolated for long periods of time. Another characteristic is that the dog, like the wolf, looks to the leader—Alpha—for direction. Both the wolf and the dog communicate through body language, not only within their pack but with outsiders.

Every pack has an Alpha figure. The dog looks to you, or should look to you, to be that leader. If your dog doesn't receive the proper training and guidance, he very well may replace you as Alpha. This would be a serious problem and is certainly a disservice to your dog.

Eye contact is one way the Alpha wolf keeps order within his pack. You are Alpha so you must establish eye contact with your puppy. Obviously your puppy will have to look at you. Practice eye contact even if you need to hold his head for five to ten seconds at a time. You can give him a treat as a reward. Make sure your eye contact is gentle and not threatening. Later, if he has been naughty, it is permissible to give him a long, penetrating look. There are some older dogs that never learned eye contact as puppies and cannot accept eye contact. You should avoid eye contact with these dogs since they feel threatened and will retaliate as such.

BODY LANGUAGE

The play bow, when the forequarters are down and the hindquarters are elevated, is an invitation to play. Puppies play fight, which helps them learn the acceptable limits of biting. This is necessary for later in their lives. Nevertheless, an owner may be falsely reassured by the playful nature of his dog's aggression. Playful aggression toward another dog or human may be an indication of serious aggression in the future. Owners should never play fight or play tug-of-war with any dog that is inclined to be dominant.

A puppy's personality will often be evident in the way he interacts with other animals. This little Eskie wants to be sure his feline friend knows he is "top dog."

Signs of submission are:
1. Avoids eye contact.
2. Active submission–the dog crouches down, ears back and the tail is lowered.
3. Passive submission–the dog

rolls on his side with his hindlegs in the air and frequently urinates.

Signs of dominance are:
1. Makes eye contact.
2. Stands with ears up, tail up and the hair raised on his neck.
3. Shows dominance over another dog by standing at right angles over it.

Dominant dogs tend to behave in characteristic ways such as:
1. The dog may be unwilling to move from his place (i.e., reluctant to give up the sofa if the owner wants to sit there).
2. He may not part with toys or objects in his mouth and may show possessiveness with his food bowl.
3. He may not respond quickly to commands.

4. He may be disagreeable for grooming and dislikes to be petted.

Dogs are popular because of their sociable nature. Those that have contact with humans during the first 12 weeks of life regard them as a member of their own species—their pack. All dogs have the potential for both dominant and submissive behavior. Only through experience and training do they learn to whom it is appropriate to show which behavior. Not all dogs are concerned with dominance but owners need to be aware of that potential. It is wise for the owner to establish his dominance early on.

A human can express dominance or submission toward a dog in the following ways:

1. Meeting the dog's gaze signals dominance. Averting the gaze signals submission. If the dog growls or threatens, averting the gaze is the first avoiding action to take—it may prevent attack. It is important to establish eye contact in the puppy. The older dog that has not been exposed to eye contact may see it as a threat and will not be willing to submit.

2. Being taller than the dog signals dominance; being lower signals submission. This is why, when attempting to make friends with a strange dog or catch the runaway, one should kneel down to his level. Some owners see their dogs become dominant when allowed on the furniture or on the bed. Then he is at the owner's level.

3. An owner can gain dominance by ignoring all the dog's social initiatives. The owner pays attention to the dog only when he obeys a command.

No dog should be allowed to achieve dominant status over any adult or child. Ways of preventing are as follows:

1. Handle the puppy gently, especially during the three- to four-month period.
2. Let the children and adults handfeed him and

Although some traits are inherited within a breed, every Eskie is an individual. This lovely pair agrees!

teach him to take food without lunging or grabbing.

3. Do not allow him to chase children or joggers.

4. Do not allow him to jump on people or mount their legs.

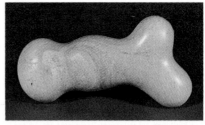

The Galileo™ is the toughest nylon bone ever made. It is flavored to appeal to your American Eskimo Dog and has a relatively soft outer layer. It is a necessary chew toy and doggy pacifier.

An unwillingness to give up his toys may signal that your dog is displaying dominant tendencies. Your Eskie must always know that you are the boss.

Even females may be inclined to mount. It is not only a male habit.

5. Do not allow him to growl for any reason.

6. Don't participate in wrestling or tug-of-war games.

7. Don't physically punish puppies for aggressive behavior. Restrain him from repeating the infraction and teach an alternative behavior. Dogs should earn everything they receive from their owners. This would include sitting to receive petting or treats, sitting before going out the door and sitting to receive the collar and leash. These types of exercises reinforce the owner's dominance.

Young children should never be left alone with a dog. It is important that children learn some basic obedience commands so they have some control over the dog. They will gain the respect of their dog.

FEAR

One of the most common problems dogs experience is being fearful. Some dogs are more afraid than others. On the lesser side, which is sometimes humorous to watch, dogs can be afraid of a strange object. They act silly when something is out of place in the house. We call his problem perceptive intelligence. He realizes the abnormal within his known environment. He does not react the same way in strange environments since he does not know what is normal.

On the more serious side is a fear of people. This can result in backing off, seeking his own space and saying "leave me alone" or it can result in an aggressive behavior that may lead to challenging the person. Respect that the dog wants to be left alone and give him time to come forward. If you approach the cornered dog, he may resort to snapping. If you leave him alone, he may decide to come forward, which should be rewarded with a treat.

Some dogs may initially be too fearful to take treats. In these cases it is helpful to make sure the dog hasn't eaten for about 24 hours. Being a little hungry encourages him to accept the treats, especially if they are of the "gourmet" variety.

A stable, even-tempered American Eskimo Dog is one that is neither fearful nor aggressive.

It is important to remember that your Eskie wants to please you, and with patience he will learn what you have to teach him!

Dogs can be afraid of numerous things, including loud noises and thunderstorms. Invariably the owner rewards (by comforting) the dog when it shows signs of fearfulness. When your dog is frightened, direct his attention to something else and act happy. Don't dwell on his fright.

AGGRESSION

Some different types of aggression are: predatory, defensive, dominance, possessive, protective, fear induced, noise provoked, "rage" syndrome (unprovoked aggression), maternal and aggression directed toward other dogs. Aggression is the most common behavioral problem encountered. Protective breeds are expected to be more aggressive than others but with the proper upbringing they can make very dependable companions. You need to be able to read your dog.

Many factors contribute to aggression including genetics and environment. An improper environment, which may include the living conditions, lack of social life, excessive punishment, being attacked or frightened by an aggressive dog, etc., can all influence a dog's behavior. Even spoiling him and giving too much praise may be detrimental. Isolation and the lack of human contact or exposure to frequent teasing by children or adults also can ruin a good dog.

Lack of direction, fear, or confusion lead to aggression in those dogs that are so inclined. Any obedience exercise, even the sit and down, can direct the dog and overcome fear and/or confusion. Every dog should learn these commands as a youngster, and there should be periodic reinforcement.

When a dog is showing signs of aggression, you should speak calmly (no screaming or hysterics) and firmly give a command that he understands, such as the sit. As soon as your dog obeys, you have assumed your dominant position. Aggression presents a problem because there may be danger to others. Sometimes it is an emotional issue. Owners may consciously or unconsciously encourage their dog's aggression. Other owners show responsibility by accepting the problem and taking measures to keep it under control. The owner is responsible for his dog's actions, and it is not wise to take a chance on someone being bitten, especially a child. Euthanasia is the solution for some owners and in severe cases this may be the best choice. However, few dogs are that dangerous and very few are that much of a threat to their owners. If caution is exercised and professional help is gained early on, most cases can be controlled.

Some authorities recommend feeding a lower protein (less than 20 percent) diet. They believe this can aid in reducing aggression. If the dog loses weight, then vegetable oil can be added. Veterinarians and behaviorists are having some success with pharmacology. In many cases treatment is possible and can improve the situation.

If you have done everything according to "the book" regarding training and socializing and are still having a behavior problem, don't procrastinate. It is important that the problem gets attention before it is out of hand. It is estimated that 20 percent of a veterinarian's time may be devoted to dealing with problems before they become so intolerable that the dog is separated from its home and owner. If your veterinarian isn't able to help, he should refer you to a behaviorist.

SUGGESTED READING

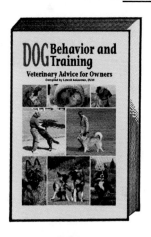

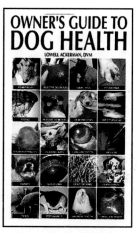

TS-252
Dog Behavior and
Training
292 pages, over 200
full-color photos

TS-249
Owner's Guide to Dog
Health
224 pages, over 190
full-color photos

TS-257
Choosing A Dog For Life
384 pages, over 700 full-
color photos

RE 334
Guide to Owning an
American Eskimo
64 pages, over 70 full-
color photos

INDEX